T0153520

THE BUDDHA IN JAIL

Cuong

The Buddha in Jail

Restoring Lives, Finding Hope and Freedom

CUONG LU

FOREWORD BY JOAN HALIFAX

OR Books
New York · London

Library of Congress Cataloging-in-Publication Data: A catalog record for this book is available from the Library of Congress.
British Library Cataloging in Publication Data: A catalog record for this book is available from the British Library.

Typeset by Lapiz Digital.

Published by OR Books in partnership with Counterpoint Press.
Distributed to the trade by Publishers Group West.

hardcover ISBN 978-1-949017-13-7 • ebook ISBN 978-1-949017-14-4

Foreword

Cuong Lu was born in Vietnam in 1968 and emigrated with his family to Holland when he was eleven. He was a monk at Plum Village, Thich Nhat Hanh's community in France, for sixteen years before returning home and becoming one of the first Buddhist prison chaplains in the Netherlands. In *The Buddha in Jail*, Cuong shares his stories and teachings in the Dutch prison system, working with hardened criminals, mostly by sitting with them in deep presence. He was able to do that because he recognized the humanness and vulnerability of each of these very tough men.

In the mid-1990s, a student of mine who was a psychologist at the Penitentiary of New Mexico, invited me to join her in her work there, and we taught meditation, council practice, and yoga for six years in maximum security and on death row. All the men we worked with had killed people. They were mostly gang members, men who had suffered extreme abuse as a result of indescribable upbringings and social marginalization. Some were mentally ill.

I recognized right away that in the presence of such suffering, one has to have impeccable integrity. Prison is complicated; it's a culture in itself. Most of the guests of the correctional system and staff come from the same communities. For me, being involved was life-changing. I learned so much about hope and hopelessness, anger and kindness, privilege and the lack of privilege. And I had a breakthrough of insight. Looking deeply, I was able to see each inmate not as an object of fear-based projections, but as a man suffering from a horrific life history, a wounded buddha.

My colleague Fleet Maull, who was incarcerated for fourteen years on charges of drug trafficking, describes practicing meditation in prison. Prison is a tough environment, he notes, where greed, hatred, and delusion are the order of the day. Yet he writes in his book *Dharma in Hell*, "I'm thoroughly convinced after spending fourteen years in prison with murderers, rapists, bank robbers, child molesters, tax dodgers, drug dealers, and every sort of criminal imaginable, that the fundamental nature of all human beings is good." Like Fleet, I believe that redemption is possible and that every situation has within it something that can teach us and lead us to our natural wisdom.

Cuong also realized right away that when the men inside were able to sit quietly, in spacious dialogue with him or in sitting meditation, alone or with the prison sangha, and were able to feel their own pain—including from childhood trauma, problematic relations, and remorse for crimes they committed—knowing and feeling the truth, even when painful, can be a source of happiness. When the inmates he worked with felt listened to, understood, and not judged, it transformed their sense of who they are, and as a result, their attitudes and behaviors changed. Throughout the book, Cuong reframes the Buddha's first noble truth of the presence of suffering, seeing the glass as half-full. Facing suffering, he says, getting beneath defenses and resistance to non-denial of even our most painful memories and experiences, can in itself be a source of happiness. He not only posits this, but he also offers example after example of transformations brought about by practicing the first noble truth this way, facing our suffering.

Let us read these stories carefully, a few at a time, and apply them to encounters we've had with those who acted badly, those we don't particularly like, and with ourselves, for all these dialogues are taking place within each of us all the time.

— *Roshi Joan Halifax*
Upaya Zen Center, Santa Fe, New Mexico
Fall 2018

Introduction

I was born in Nha Trang, a coastal resort city in southern Vietnam known for its beaches, diving, and offshore islands. When I was a child, my brothers, sisters, and I walked to the beach every morning and swam in the warm waters of the Pacific Ocean until the sun rose, which was at about 6 a.m. Then we walked home together, ate breakfast, and went to school. Our life was peaceful, or so it seemed. But the country was at war, and behind our peacefulness was violence, not just in the gunfire among warring parties, but everywhere. At school, we played war, fighting to see who was strongest. For us, it was a game. I never really knew peace in Vietnam, even in our idyllic, coastal home in Nha Trang.

In 1975, North and South Vietnam were reunited. The fighting ended, but fear persisted. Fear is always a product of war, and in our case, each side anticipated revenge from the other. In 1979, my family fled the country. I was eleven and had no idea why we left.

We arrived safely in Hong Kong, and were held there, along with thousands of others, in a huge barn that had just one small window. Hygiene was poor, and people were dying of curable illnesses. I heard adults say, "The price of freedom is high," and I didn't understand. Then one day I was allowed to sit by the small window, and I saw a little girl on her way to school. I wanted to go to school like her. That was my simple idea of freedom.

After a year of waiting, we were allowed to resettle in the Netherlands. I went to school, but I wasn't free. I brought the war with me. I fought with my Dutch classmates to show I was the strongest. I thought they were afraid of me until one day, a lovely boy my own age said to me, "We don't need to fight, Cuong, we're friends." His words pierced me like a thunderbolt. "We're friends"—a concept I'd never known or even imagined. For the first time, I sensed the difference between war and peace.

Another time I told my teacher, "Mr. van der Sterre, you're too nice. We're not afraid of you." I meant he wasn't a good teacher. He immediately replied, "Cuong, why should you be afraid of me? We're friends." Again, I was disarmed.

In 1987, my mother heard that Zen master Thich Nhat Hanh was coming to Holland to lead a meditation retreat, and she asked me to attend with her. When I saw Thich Nhat Hanh, I was profoundly touched by his presence. I had never seen a peaceful Vietnamese man before. I was among the youngest in the group of twenty-five Vietnamese refugees and could see the older folks stuck in their anger and frustration. Thich Nhat Hanh had obviously found peace. My mother and I needed a role model, and he won our trust. I saw in him an elder brother who could show me the way. My mother observed my response and said, "Thich Nhat Hanh is your teacher."

He taught us conscious breathing, to kiss the earth with our feet as we walked, to "be peace" in every moment. I practiced that way for a week and came home a different person. I continued to practice what he'd taught—day and night, breathing and smiling—and my mother expressed her disapproval. In Vietnam, only monastics practice meditation, and she said to me, "Cuong, you're not a monk!" Her words awakened me. I wanted to become a monk, just like Thich Nhat Hanh. I wanted to be peace.

I received a diploma in computer science in 1992, and rather than go to work to earn money, I decided to learn more about my culture and myself. I went to the University of Leiden and majored in Asian Studies. That September, Thich Nhat Hanh came to Holland to lead another retreat, and a month later I took a train to France and visited Plum Village, Thich Nhat Hanh's practice community. There I saw a peaceful Vietnam in miniature. The residents— monks, nuns, and laypeople, Vietnamese and people from around the world—were peaceful and happy. They called Thich Nhat Hanh Thây (*teacher* in Vietnamese). Soon after that, I left university to study peace at Plum Village under the guidance of Thich Nhat Hanh. I stayed for sixteen years.

Thây gave two lectures a week. On the other days, we were encouraged to apply his teachings in everyday activities. We did sitting meditation, walking meditation, work meditation, cooking meditation, living each moment in mindfulness. It all sat well with me. When the temple gong sounded, everyone stopped and practiced three mindful breaths. I flourished in that environment of peace. One day in a lecture, Thây said, "Come home, my child. Don't be a hungry ghost." I burst into tears. After the talk, I went to him and said, "I want to come home." He understood and put both his hands on my head. The following year, I was ordained a Buddhist monk.

I didn't always have an easy time with my teacher. I admired him, but I also thought there were ways he could have explained his wisdom more clearly. And my own creative impulses were chafing at the bit. After seven years in Plum Village, in the year 2000, I received recognition as a teacher in Thây's lineage in a Lamp Transmission Ceremony.

Three years later, I began teaching the Dharma. I taught that happiness is the first truth. This is a radically different expression of the Buddha's First Noble Truth—*dukkha-satya*—which is usually translated as "there is suffering." But while practicing at Plum Village, I discovered that happiness is available when you know who you are and no longer have the illusion of a separate self, when you recognize the penetrating interconnection between yourself and all of life. That insight gave me hope and direction, and I wanted to share it. I saw that I could help others overcome loneliness, as I had, and find meaning again in their lives.

In 2009, I left Plum Village to follow my dream of teaching and having a family. My first year outside the monastery was difficult. It took time getting used to being in society. Then one night in 2010, in the midst of duress and confusion, I suddenly understood the nature of suffering and the nature of happiness—that they're both empty, and they're interdependent. Suffering is happiness, and happiness is suffering. This experience gave me a new lease on life, and I decided to teach the Dharma in the Netherlands. At first people came to me out of curiosity, and eventually they saw that as a former monk, now a layman, I was able to relate to their lives and explain the Dharma in ways they found accessible.

In 2011, I was hired by the Dutch government as a prison chaplain, responsible for the care of prisoners in four jails, three of which are near my home in Gouda in the province of South Holland. Together with five colleagues, I was present at the launch of the Netherlands' Department of Spiritual Care recognizing Buddhism as an official denomination, along with Catholicism, Protestantism, Judaism, Hinduism, Islam, and humanism.

Every prisoner in the Netherlands has the right to an hour of spiritual care a week, and every prison has a nondenominational "Silent Center." So I was able to use the Silent Center in each of the four prisons every week for meditation and one-on-one pastoral counseling.

In a short time, I saw that prison offered an opportunity for these men to experience real happiness. They were there, I felt, looking for the happiness they'd never found. It was profoundly satisfying to watch them discover that "happiness is a truth." They understood this teaching perfectly and found, in prison, a happiness deeper than money, power, or sex—a happiness that is always there for them. Until then, they'd felt alienated, disconnected, and lonely, and many of them were there because they'd committed horrendous crimes while in that lost state. News began to spread, and the department that prepares prisoners to reenter society invited me to teach in their program as well.

At the beginning of my chaplaincy, most of the prisoners were unable to sit still long enough to listen to my lectures. They kept interrupting me. But in a short time, they learned to sit quietly and soon began inviting other prisoners to come as well. I told them they aren't separate from their ancestors and their families, and I saw many of them smiling and crying.

The medical staff began referring prisoners to our classes, men who couldn't sleep, eat, or overcome their depression. I had to exercise patience to help them. Deep listening, mindful breathing, and deep trust were necessary to help them to discover themselves and be happy again.

What surprised me the most was not what I was able to offer the prisoners, but what I received from them. They confirmed for me that "happiness is a truth" and that touching our own suffering is, in itself, a source of relief and happiness. I cared for seventy prisoners in the four facilities. In this book, I share my joy, and their joy. I still find it unbelievable that I was able to connect so quickly and deeply with these folks who were considered by society to be hardened criminals. It might be, in part, because my own upbringing in a war zone prepared me to meet them in their pain and work with them to touch what is deep and true.

Life is full of surprises—criminals can become Buddhas when we touch their pain with insight. I saw and experienced their transformation and joyfulness, and for this I am grateful. When I left the chaplaincy in 2017, my wife encouraged me to write this book for prisoners and others in deep pain, to help everyone discover a way to be peace.

— Cuong Lu
Gouda, the Netherlands
Fall 2018

1 .

"What do you think is the worst part of being in jail?" a prisoner named Derek asked me, and before I could respond, he said, "You don't have the key to your own cell. A guard locks you in, walks away, and you have to wait till he comes back." I understood. Confined by four walls, locked in a cell, you feel powerless.

The Buddha taught that we're all imprisoned by body and mind. Because we don't understand our true nature, we feel unhappy and unfree. For a prisoner, it's difficult to see that you're incarcerated not only in your cell, but—even more so—by not realizing that freedom is, first of all, an attitude. The Dharma, the Buddha's teaching of awakening, offers us a key to free ourselves, whether we're locked in prison or in the confines of our narrow views.

For six years, I had the opportunity to bring the Dharma into prisons, and what I witnessed and experienced was a wake-up call for me. I learned that even in the darkest places, people could live happily and free. Thanks to the Dharma, I saw prisoners find freedom while still incarcerated and experience joy for the first time in their lives. I met the Buddha in jail. I discovered that each prisoner is a Buddha, capable of awakening. In Vietnamese we say, "Once you drop the butcher's knife, you become a Buddha." There's no difference between a butcher, a prisoner, and a Buddha.

2 .

Each morning when I went to work as a prison chaplain, I had to pass through thirteen electric doors just to reach my office. At each door, I pushed a button and waited. Often it took a few minutes for a guard to see me on the closed-circuit TV and open the door; and so at each door, I had a chance to practice patience and stand at the mercy of others, like the prisoners. Most of us take for granted that we can open and close our own doors. They may be unlocked, but even if they're locked, we have the key. Prisoners don't have the keys to open the doors to their cells. They're dependent on the guards.

For many of the prisoners I met, the doors of their lives were closed, some starting the day they were born. Listening to their stories, I saw how choices they made got them into trouble. Most knew little happiness. One man was abandoned by his mother, a prostitute, and his father, a drug addict, and when he was thirteen, he began breaking into cars at night to sleep. Later he became a professional car thief.

3.

I've been a Dharma teacher for twenty years, and I've observed that prisoners, war veterans, refugees, and others who have been through extreme difficulties are often able to understand the Dharma more quickly than those whose lives have been easier. Sometimes I witnessed a deep understanding of the Dharma at our first meeting. In just twenty minutes, they tuned in to a profound happiness, a joy in body and mind they'd never felt before. These are people who had touched the bottom of their suffering. Once they could see the suffering they were clinging to, thanks to remaining still in the presence of trauma, many were able to release the hold their suffering had on them and experience a profound happiness.

Once you taste that depth, you will never forget it. It changes you. One prisoner told me, "I've never been as happy as this. If I had discovered the Dharma earlier, I wouldn't be in prison now. I had no idea happiness was this close. I've been looking for relief my whole life, and the more I looked, the more I suffered. I made many mistakes—running after suffering thinking it was happiness."

One fellow chaplain told me, "We don't have Buddhists in this prison. People in the Netherlands are Christian." I replied, "Well, now there's one," and they began to call me "the Buddhist." What that chaplain conveyed was that the prisoners, guards, and others in the system didn't know anything about Buddhism. So, slowly, I taught a few prisoners to quiet their minds through meditation and offered basic teachings on the consequences of thoughts and actions and Buddhist precepts, and they began to look forward to our meetings. When I was away, even for a short time, someone would ask, "Where's the Buddha?"

The first time I heard this, I was taken aback. The historical Buddha is said to have been a perfectly enlightened being, and I surely am not. Then I began to see that everyone, every prisoner, every warden, and every chaplain is the Buddha. The potential to wake up to the way things are dwells deeply in each of us.

4 .

Looking without prejudice, seeing things as they are, is an important Buddhist practice. One day, a prisoner came to me and said, "Mr. Buddhist, I want to join your group." I asked, "Are you a Buddhist?" "No, sir," he replied. "I'm not. But can I join your meditation group?"

"Of course you can," I told him. "But may I ask why you want to practice meditation?"

"Because I see the way you look at us. I see that in your eyes we're not just prisoners. You don't discriminate. It's wonderful to be seen that way. It gives me confidence in myself, and I want to learn from you." He paused, then continued, "Not only the way you look, but also the way you walk. You radiate peace when you walk in the prison. Nobody else walks that way. I see both prisoners and staff holding a lot of sorrow and anxiety as they walk. I can see the worries in their minds. I have lots of worries too, and I want to learn how to walk, how to *be* without worrying. Then he added another reason. "I've been watching the guys who meditate with you. They're more peaceful than the rest of us. I want to learn that, too."

His eloquence touched me. Learning to be peaceful is a practice. I asked his name, and he said, "Andrew." "Andrew, from now on you are my student. I'm going to teach you to be peaceful, like the Buddha." I could see he was happy for my support, but he didn't quite believe me. He was agitated, so I asked him to sit with me quietly. "I can't," he said. "I have ADHD." I encouraged him to try, and at the end of the sitting, despite his fidgeting, I said, "You did very well." I said it from my heart, and he was surprised. He hadn't sat quietly, but he did sit. He stood up one time, but he didn't walk away. Andrew was a fighter, and I respected his strength. When I expressed my respect, he glowed with satisfaction.

5.

Colleagues thought prisoners came to me for free time, a chance to get outside their cells. I don't think that's the case. Sitting quietly for a half hour is never easy, and certainly not for these men. It was a big effort for them. They didn't come for fun, but to learn something practical. Many would have given up, but I recognized their effort and encouraged them. The change in each was clear to see. They became quieter and more peaceful. I was happy that they trusted me. Trust in a teacher on a path of self-knowing is very important.

One day, Andrew came to me and said, "I've nearly served my time, so I'm allowed home visits on weekends. On the train home last weekend, I didn't do anything. I just sat there and looked at the beautiful scenery outside. I've never done that before. I felt so peaceful."

6.

Prisons are generally unhappy places. Prisoners want their time inside to pass quickly, or more precisely, they want to forget about time. So I invited them to get in touch with *timelessness*, which is a vast dimension of freedom. Being free in prison is possible. Being happy in prison is possible.

Many used drugs to forget their misery. It didn't help, or if it did, it helped only a little. The problems always returned. Meditation doesn't help you forget your misery. In fact, it helps you feel the truth of your unhappiness and thus remember what life is. Life is not a matter of time. Time is a product of wrong thinking. When wrong thinking becomes still, our life becomes an expression of timeless wonder. Prisoners who learn the art of sitting also learn to quiet their thinking, and they experience a happiness deeper than drugs. One man told me, "Cuong, this is better than a joint."

After learning meditation and practicing daily, many stopped using drugs. They became friendlier toward each other and dealt more easily with their anger. They experienced happiness not just in their minds, but also in their bodies. One prisoner showed me his fingernails and said, "Cuong, they're growing again!" Our bodies have their own wisdom and respond to our states of mind. This man's fingernails had stopped growing when he felt his life was over. Renewed growth is a sign of happiness, and he touched his life anew.

7.

After attending a few sessions of our meditation group, a prisoner named Fred asked to speak with me, so I invited him for a cup of tea. Fred was a Christian minister who had murdered his wife. He looked as though he might burst into tears as he began to speak, "During meditation, Cuong, I experienced joy, not just in my mind but also in my body. I heard my body say, 'I'm happy. Life is beautiful. I want to *live*.' My body doesn't lie, and this was the first encouraging message I've had in a long time. It's funny; I was a minister for thirty years."

I listened deeply, carefully following my breathing. He continued, "I want to live my life. It's a sign. As a pastor, I was miserable for a long time. Can you guess why?" He sat in silence, looking for the words to express what he meant. *"I don't believe.* For thirty years, I told people God loves them. Each time I told that to someone dying, they felt a deep peace. But I don't believe in God."

I sat completely still. What he said was familiar. Many Buddhists, even Dharma teachers, don't believe in the Buddha's insight, which is a foundation of Buddhism. I asked whether he had told anyone, and he replied, "Once I told a group of ministers, and I saw the panic in their eyes. It's taboo to say that. You can feel a lack of faith, but you can't say it."

"Why not?" I asked.

"I touched their pain. Many of them also don't believe, but they have to do their job. So they lie. I lied for thirty years."

Spontaneously I responded, "I don't think you lied. When you told dying men and women that God loves them, it was the truth. You loved them, and they felt it. What you didn't realize is that God is within you."

Reverend Fred began to cry. "No one in my denomination says that, not even in seminary. Why did I have to suffer so long?" For the first time, he believed in God, sitting in God's presence and the presence of himself.

8 .

Over the years, many priests and ministers have told me they don't believe. I've listened with empathy while thinking that belief is not difficult. In a short time, perhaps twenty minutes, anyone can regain faith in himself. Belief in yourself is critical, especially for those who suffer deeply. Suffering isn't the worst thing; not believing in yourself is. It's like not believing in happiness. After discovering happiness in his body, Fred quickly experienced healing. Wounds that had been unattended for years began to heal.

Without faith, Fred didn't have direction. For him, life was survival. Most prisoners I met feel the same. They hadn't learned to live, just to fight and survive. It was true for me, too. I came to Holland with mental health problems. I had never seen peace in my country, and when I arrived in Holland, a country at peace, I kept on fighting to survive. I was looking for problems and got into fights. When another boy said to me, "Don't fight, Cuong, we're friends," the word *friend* became linked in my mind with the words *don't fight*. It was a beautiful lesson, and I recognized my weakness.

It was easy for me to recognize the survival instinct in prisoners. Exhausted and suicidal, Fred was tired of lying to survive. By practicing meditation, he discovered joy for the first time in his life. Without the joy of life, we might commit a crime. Fred murdered his wife. Some prison chaplains get worn down by the work. I had the opportunity to guide prisoners to experience the joy of life, and to do so, I had to stay fully present and embody the energy of joy.

9.

When I began my chaplaincy, I encouraged the men attending the meditation program to bring friends with them. "We don't have friends here," they told me, "only fellow prisoners."

But over time, that changed. The men became friendly to each other, in the Silent Room and in their units as well. Respect is the ground of friendship. As these prisoners developed respect for themselves, they became more respectful of each other.

One man observed that after some of the prisoners in his unit began meditating, there was less violence. They worked well together and helped each other. One man said to me, "Even the fag in our unit is left alone in peace. He's accepted now; that's great to see."

Another prisoner asked if he could meditate with me every morning. I was responsible for men in four prisons, so it wasn't possible. Each prisoner can join our meditations once a week. When I was absent, they missed the support.

10.

For an hour each week, prisoners in our meditation classes were reminded of their own value. I treated each man with respect. I believed in their capacity to be awakened. They showed me their ability to learn and understand Buddhism in a short time, because they knew suffering and appreciated peace. In the Buddha's first Dharma talk, he described suffering as the first truth. Seeing our suffering is the starting point. We have a lot of suffering in ourselves, but we choose not to see it clearly. Instead, we just hold onto it. Recognizing our suffering is difficult. We blame others. We don't see that suffering is a choice.

Suffering takes many forms. One is guilt about what we've done in the past. That feeling can haunt us at night. When we don't sleep well, we might take pills. In prison, nighttime is especially disturbing. Some prisoners kick on the doors of their cells. Even though their suffering shows up so clearly at night, during the day they don't see it. They display machismo, power. One prisoner told me, "If they see you're weak, they'll abuse you." Prisoners regard suffering as a weakness.

I told the meditators that suffering isn't a weakness. Those who can see their own suffering are strong. When anyone comes to me, there's always space for them to see and feel their suffering. When you sit quietly in silence, you get stronger. You stop denying and fighting against your suffering. An hour not fighting against your own suffering is a lot.

11.

Many people see suffering as the enemy of happiness, but that's not true. Suffering and happiness coexist, and being able to see suffering is, in fact, already happiness. Instead of calling suffering the first truth, I like to say that happiness is the first truth. If prisoners can be happy for an hour a week, so can we. Periods of happiness, even short-lived, are energizing. Prisoners would come into the meditation hall enraged and leave delighted. For an hour, they could be themselves and believe in themselves, which is the basis of healing.

Through experiences like these, suffering began to lose its power over them, and many were able to sleep through the night.

The prison health service referred a fair number of people to our meditation class. That's how Manuel joined us. He couldn't sleep; he heard voices and saw ghosts. I offered him instruction in meditation and suggested he feel his feelings. But he couldn't, he couldn't feel anything. I always tried to help prisoners get in touch with at least one feeling during their first hour; it helped them appreciate the practicality of meditation. But Manuel couldn't. I didn't give up, and neither did he.

Suddenly, in the third week, he was able to contact his ancestors, and from that moment, he was freed from nighttime suffering. He no longer saw ghosts or heard voices, and he began to sleep well. It was a miracle. He could approach his wounds and tell his story. His ancestors were Moluccans, the indigenous inhabitants of a small group of islands that are now part of Indonesia. The Moluccans fought with the Dutch in Indonesia's civil war and came to Holland afterward, waiting for the Dutch government to grant them independence. But it didn't happen. Manuel grew up in that environment, experiencing injustice firsthand. His suffering was also the suffering of his ancestors, and his breakthrough was also the breakthrough of his ancestors. He was seventy when he discovered happiness, and he began to carry himself with newfound confidence. He began bringing other prisoners to our group, and they called him Grandpa Manuel.

For prisoners who receive guidance, prison can be a place of transformation. But this doesn't happen often, and even in a liberal country like Holland, prisons often focus on retribution. Of course, prison is for punishment, but to solve individual and social problems, prisoners need guidance. Without it, they often revert to old habits after they're released. Prison offers us a chance to help those in trouble, and it's to everyone's benefit to capitalize on that chance.

Many inmates told me the worst thing they experienced in prison was not being able to be with their loved ones, not being able to watch their kids grow up. The isolation of detention is the worst punishment. Many prisoners grew up in isolation and loneliness. It's important for them to have contact with home. When there is contact, there is happiness. Prisoners spend a lot of money calling home; prison payphones are shockingly expensive. In large and small ways, we can help those who have gotten into trouble by encouraging more training and classes for prisoners, and by asking legislators to reduce prison phone rates.

From the moment Manuel made contact with his ancestors, he touched his deepest happiness. Through meditation, we reconnect with ourselves and others, both visible and invisible. Happiness means freedom from loneliness.

1 2 .

Peter was eighteen when he was arrested for pimping and dealing. A group of girls worked for him in an operation overseen by his uncle. When I met him in prison, Peter was twenty. He described giving drugs to the girls and watching them become addicted. "When you're addicted," he said, "you don't have freedom. I learned that from my family. Many of these girls were from nice families, and after they were addicted, they'd do anything. It was easy. With drugs, I could control them." He told me he'd been taking in $12,000 a month. What did an eighteen-year-old do with that kind of money? "I went on vacations, bought expensive cars, hung out in high-end brothels."

I asked whether he was happy when he had all that money. He thought for a moment, then said, "I thought I was, but one day I noticed how emaciated one of the girls had become. She was addicted and didn't look human anymore. She had been a beautiful girl, and I turned her into a ghost. I stole her life and her beauty. When I saw her suffering, I saw my own and decided to stop being a pimp." At such a young age, he woke up. I can still hear him saying, "Her suffering was my suffering."

In Buddhism, we call that *interbeing*. We're not just individuals. We don't exist separately. I am you, and you are me. Becoming free of a wrong perception can be a source of joy. Peter's life was extreme, but through it he discovered that he had made his money, derived his happiness, from other people's suffering. In our own ways, we too run after money to try to buy happiness. We consume products based on the suffering of others.

Men like Peter don't share their stories easily. You have to gain their confidence. As a chaplain, I could offer confidentiality; I didn't have to report what the prisoners told me. But that wasn't enough. I had to meet them without judgment, without thinking that I'm more righteous than they are. We often believe we're better than others. As long as there are two separate people facing each other, listening isn't possible. The separation needs to dissolve so that the two of you become one body, one being. Only then will a prisoner tell you his story. Interbeing is the basis of love and compassion.

As a chaplain, every day I went to work happy, and I could share my happiness with the prisoners just by showing up. When they saw me, they could feel it, and it brought them comfort. That was enough; I didn't have to do anything. They trusted me. I felt no judgment and trusted the best in them, knowing that the best in a prisoner is not less than the best in the Buddha. Buddhists believe that everyone has Buddha nature. I could see that truth every day, and I was grateful for it. You can't buy that with money. Prisoners gave me the most valuable gift, their trust.

13.

A prisoner named Joe told me, "Everyone on the outside judges us, Cuong."

When you enter prison, you get a registration number, and Joe had his number tattooed on his forehead. I asked why he did that, and he said, "Every time I leave here, people avoid me. They cross the street to keep their distance or look down if I enter a shop. So, I figured, why should I hide that I'm a convict?" He asked if I understood, and I told him, "Not really. This is difficult to hear."

"Come downtown with me and stand behind me, and you'll see how much I scare people. I try to blend in, but it never works, so finally I accepted my fate and tattooed my prison reg number right on my face."

Even when walking down the street, these men are still in prison. The walls of the society are impermeable—composed of prejudice and fear— and they keep out those who are different. Through isolation and loneliness, prisoners' self-confidence gets damaged, and the job of a chaplain is to help them rebuild it. I always encourage them to stop judging themselves and to stop calling each other "criminals."

It's astonishing to see how easily they're able to become free with only a little meditation practice and Dharma teaching. They're used to looking at the world horizontally—east, west, north, and south. I encouraged them to make a vertical connection as well, to connect with their ancestors. We all come from somewhere. Joe believed he would be a prisoner his whole life. But if he could see himself vertically, he would know he's more than a prisoner. He's also his ancestors. Tuning in to the vertical connection, he'd see that his ancestors don't have reg numbers on their foreheads. When prisoners make a vertical connection, they discover how to be free from prison, even while serving time.

14.

Violence can result from a lack of self-confidence. It's difficult to see this, but when we stop believing in ourselves, we start treating others badly as well. Believing in oneself is, at the same time, believing in others. Those who are violent often have a hard time believing they have a right to exist.

Keith got into fights in the streets and in pubs, and had run-ins with the police. He didn't understand why he kept doing that; he didn't like the way his life was going. So, he asked to speak with me.

We began with deep breathing and deep listening. Keith told me he had served in the army as a UN Peacekeeper, helping countries torn by conflict create conditions for a lasting peace. But his authority was limited, and there were times he was unable to protect innocent people. He requested a transfer to a special unit where he wouldn't need permission to kill perpetrators. Over time, he killed ninety-two people.

He was married when he entered the army. He wasn't home much, although he did send money to his wife. But he wasn't there when she had emotional problems. He was abroad fighting when she got sick and died.

In our first talk, he told me he'd been abused by his aunt when he was six-years-old. He was surprised we touched on that subject in our first conversation. "I've been to more than twenty shrinks, and we've never gotten this far. How did you do that, Cuong?

I asked him, "Why did you share things you never told your therapists?"

He thought a little and said, "Because they were doing a job, and I could feel it. Some of them looked at their watches while they were talking with me. They had to finish with me to see their next client. You listen with your heart."

When he was six, his parents divorced, and his father wasn't available to give him the attention he needed. His aunt showed up and gave him pocket money. She played games with him, and she spoiled him. Then she asked him to massage her and came on to him sexually. He didn't understand, but did what she asked. In the bathroom, she peed on his face. He didn't like it, but his aunt told him it was a game. The worst for him was when she sat on his face and began to rub. He couldn't breathe and almost suffocated. It excited her when he couldn't breathe, Keith said, and she climaxed. Of course, he didn't understand what was happening. Then, at a certain point, his father forbade him from seeing his aunt anymore. He didn't understand why, but he'd never told his secret to anyone.

As he grew up, he couldn't find love. For him, love was a kind of sexual game. When he was fourteen, he touched his girlfriend's body the way he'd learned from his aunt, and she didn't like it. Love became harder and harder to find.

Keith wasn't happy in his marriage. He hardly saw his wife and two children. He was always on the battlefield, and his constant running away continued until our conversation. Suddenly he could feel and see what had happened. We met the following week and the week after that, and I suggested he write a letter to his aunt. He found it really difficult. His aunt was still alive, and I made it clear he didn't have to send the letter, just write it. The exercise helped him relive those horrible moments and at the same time, to see them with the eyes of an adult. As a child, he didn't know how to deal with feelings he couldn't understand. Everything was buried and couldn't be transformed. It ran his life. Writing that letter was liberating. It took a lot of effort, but it was worth it. By writing, he could better understand himself, his aunt, and much of his life. After that, his face began to shine, revealing more and more happiness. He also experienced deep rest during sitting meditation.

Finally, he forgave his aunt. "What she did was evil. There was suffering for both of us. In my writing and in my meditation, I can see that now. Forgiving her, I feel free. There's a softness inside me I never felt before."

I asked, "Do you have regrets?"

He said, "I'm sorry I wasn't a better husband, that I couldn't be there for my wife. I only sent her money, and that was never enough. She needed love, but I didn't have it to give her."

"It's not too late," I suggested.

"But my wife passed away, Cuong."

"Yes, but your children are still alive. You can take care of them."

He was happy to hear this. "Yes, I have a chance to make it right."

"It's never too late to wake up. You've been in a deep sleep. New opportunities are now available, starting with enjoying your children. You can express your love for your wife and yourself in the way you are with them."

15.

After some months leading guided meditations in prison, I could feel the atmosphere change. The prisoners began to enter the room with more peace and silence. When they spoke to each other, they were less angry. Before we began meditating, I always served tea and cookies and made sure a stick of incense was burning, the floor was clean, and the meditation cushions had been placed carefully on the floor. It's important to prepare a nice atmosphere. We often think meditation is an individual exercise, but it's not. We do it together.

I told the prisoners, "It's as though we're in a boat together, going in the direction of happiness and freedom. You don't have to do anything. You can just sit there, or you can join those who are rowing. It's up to you."

When they walked into the meditation room, they already felt peaceful. The energy was already there, and they felt it. The group grew quickly, and I had to organize a second class, this one as part of a program preparing prisoners for reentry into civilian life. Just as when I'd entered the prison system as a chaplain, when I gave my first talks in the reentry program, I was interrupted a lot. The men were clearly engaged and curious and responded quickly to the things they disagreed with. Gradually they began to listen more deeply and interrupt less. They were especially interested in the teaching of no-self. I said, "An apple isn't just an apple. It's also a pear. You are not just you. You're other folks, too." They liked that. "I am you" was not theoretical for them. I saw them applying it in their interactions with one another. They visited with each other after class, and later, after they were released, many of them stayed in touch and grew closer.

It was special to see more and more Muslims joining our class. Many said, "I need rest." The imams were open to them attending a meditation class led by a Buddhist. They gave me a lot of space to be with these Muslim prisoners. At first, the imams didn't regard Buddhism as a religion, rather as a way of life. But after a while, as they learned that wasn't quite right, they still encouraged Muslim prisoners to meditate with us. Several said to me, "You're truly our brother. Please teach us about conscious breathing. We don't have that exercise in Islam."

Buddhism is both a way of life and a religion. Thanks to its practicality and depth, I was able to bring prisoners of different backgrounds together. Together they experienced harmony, rest, and brotherhood.

16.

One day Manuel brought Raid to our group. Raid, a beautiful young man who always smiled, was a member of the Bandidos motorcycle gang. A month later, Manuel brought Karl, a Hell's Angel. Both these gangbangers called Manuel "Grandpa." Raid's ancestry was Romani, gypsy, and he always had trouble finding a home. He was a perennial outsider, and he had a difficult relationship with his wife and children. So, instead, he hung out with his friends. He was in prison because he'd "helped" some of these friends. His wife had warned him about them, but he wouldn't listen.

He was a fireball who needed cool water. In group meditation, he sat near me, and my energy cooled his inner heat. He could feel it, and Raid never missed meditation. He sat quietly, and when he left, he always said, "Thank you very much, Cuong."

Grandpa Manuel saw the change in Raid. While in the past, Raid had exploded every time he spoke to his wife on the phone, after he'd been meditating for a while, he was able to listen to her. What Manuel found even more impressive was that Raid began talking to Karl. "Rival gangbangers never talk to each other, Cuong. You can't imagine how rare this is. The differences are deep. We're in the presence of a miracle."

In a private conversation, Raid asked me, "How can I control my anger? When I'm angry, I hit and kick my children." He cried as he told me this. I looked at him and said, "You can control yourself. You can be a source of happiness for your family."

He said, "I'm so impatient, Cuong. When I'm angry, I become violent or just walk away. I'm never at home with my family. How can I learn patience?"

"You are patient, Raid," I told him. "You sit quietly next to me in the meditation hall."

He smiled. "That's because of you. I'm not patient by nature. I smile, but that's to hide my rage. My kids know it. They're afraid of my smile. I can't hide my anger from them. They know it's my weakness."

I interrupted him: "...and they love you. You don't have to hide. You're a beautiful man, Raid, inside and out. You may have chosen the wrong friends, but don't forget you still have your wife and children as wonderful companions in your life."

As Raid started to have confidence in himself, his transformation was visible. He still had fights with Karl, but he was able to let go of his anger quickly and make peace with him again. This was new to him, and it also surprised the guards.

When they were released, Manuel and his wife visited Raid's family. Raid's wife said to Manuel's wife, "I hardly recognize him. He came home a new man. He helps me at home and plays with the children. He doesn't beat the kids anymore. What happened?

17.

A transformation also took place in Karl. Many of the prisoners I met were talented, and with proper guidance could grow quickly in the direction of peace, harmony, and stability. Although not Romani, since entering adulthood Karl, too, never had a home. He traveled and experienced a lot in his life, but he never found peace. Peace is a kind of home. It's more than a nice feeling; peace is present in all feelings.

There's a difference between contact and connection. In contact, a subject searches for an object to overcome loneliness. With connection, you're already part of a something larger and don't need an object to be happy. When you taste this, you have peace. Karl experienced that peace during meditation, and it was a game changer for him. His transformation had a big effect on his sixteen-year-old daughter, Carina. Carina hated when her parents fought.

I suggested to Karl that he make a list of his wife's positive traits and start each conversation with her mentioning one of these traits. He did the same with Carina, always mentioning a positive aspect of her mother. Carina became calmer, and mother and daughter noticed characteristics in one another they hadn't noticed before.

With his newfound happiness, Karl brought other prisoners to our class. One day, he told me, "Cuong, you've helped me a lot. You're the only one here who doesn't hide behind a role. You give yourself to us. You love us and you guide us with your heart. You're surrounded by murderers and rapists, but you don't judge. And so we respect and listen to you. These are the toughest guys in society."

The thing is, I didn't see them as "tough guys." When I spoke to them, I saw young men who were able to shed long-held tears. They had tough lives. Many were abandoned and had to fend for themselves without adult guidance or protection. For some, it was easier to stay in prison than face life outside. Meditation brought many of them peace. Karl and Raid still argue with each other, and they're still members of rival gangs, but they no longer fight.

18.

Conflicts can be solved in prison. Prisoners can learn to respect themselves, each other, and life. John's story shows this, once again, thanks to meditation.

John hadn't slept for nights. A prisoner in a cell on the floor below him played loud music all night long. John tried to practice patience, but he really couldn't sleep. So one day he went to the other prisoner, explained the problem, and asked him not to play music so loud in the middle of the night. The other prisoner immediately began yelling at him. That's normal in prison culture. If he had acceded to John's request too quickly, he would have been seen as weak, and that could have horrible consequences. Weaklings are abused and extorted. He scolded John and went straight back to his cell. John yelled back and went to his cell. The rest of the prisoners held their breath. Tension was in the air, everyone could feel it. John was muscular, intelligent, and had many friends. Everyone expected a fight.

John was enraged and was planning to beat the other guy up. But when he got to his cell, he sat down and followed his breathing. He observed his anger. Later he told me, "I did what you taught us, Cuong. I didn't judge my anger. And suddenly I saw my anger for the first time. I was livid and really wanted to hurt him, but instead I sat quietly. I thought about your teaching 'doing nothing,' and I did nothing. I sat and watched my anger disappear." It was a great victory. "If I'd been able to do this before, I wouldn't be here. I'm here because I couldn't control my anger."

John left his cell and went back to the other prisoner. Everyone held their breath. They knew that John was boss of the unit. He *had* to do something, because he'd been insulted.

"I went into his cell and could see he was scared. I reached out my hand and said, 'Sorry.' He was clearly disarmed. Then he held out his hand, we shook hands, and he said: 'I'm sorry too.' And Cuong, that night the music stopped." John was proud of his victory. It was a victory in himself.

19.

A warden told me, "Cuong, I think the decrease in violence in the prison has to do with your meditation group. We have no proof, but I think it's true." She offered whatever support I needed.

John had been a major drug dealer at a young age. He got every-thing he wanted, starting with respect. For men like John, respect is most important. He had expensive clothes, fancy cars, and was always surrounded by beautiful women.

I asked, "Were you happy?" and he replied, "I went to parties, I drank a lot and did a lot of drugs. I had tons of sex. And I burned out. When I was caught, I was just twenty-one and ready to stop. In prison, I got to know you. You taught me to stay with myself. You helped me see my own value. As a dealer, I had money and power. Cuong, you know the movie *Scarface*?"

"I do. Al Pacino played drug lord Tony Montana."

John smiled, "I was a kind of Al Pacino. It was crazy. When I had a lot of money, I had big dreams, but I was never happy. Now I'm in prison. I have no money, no big dreams anymore, and I'm really happy. I'm paying attention to small things—not the big dreams, but the little things. They were always there, but I didn't see them—like conversations, smiles, meals, walks. If I hadn't been caught, I'd be dead by now. I'm glad I was arrested. For the first time, I appreciate life. Thanks to meditation, I see life as beautiful. I want to live and grow old, and I appreciate myself. I used to need respect from other people. Now I respect myself."

His words, "I respect myself," echoed in my ears. Is that what matters? Is that what prisoners want? I think so. They lacked respect for themselves. They lacked appreciation for life. They lacked the experience of happiness. They searched for happiness and missed real happiness. I had to learn the same thing when I emigrated from Vietnam. Happiness is in each of us, but we don't know it. Prisoners feel it right away; they just need an example. The people they met before—their parents, teachers, and friends—weren't happy. The first thing I tried to help prisoners experience was happiness. When I embodied happiness, they felt it. One day as I was walking past a row of cells, a man behind bars looked at me and said, "You see the light, right?"

I laughed and said, "I'm happy."

He nodded, "I can see it. Very nice."

John had seen the light within himself. For the first time, he was immersed in his own happiness. "I enjoy little things now," he told me.

2 0.

Fred, the ex-minister who didn't believe in God, hadn't experienced happiness in his life. "No one has been an example to me, Cuong. My spiritual teachers weren't happy. When I told them I wasn't a believer, they flipped out and asked me never to speak about it again. So I learned to keep my mouth shut. But I couldn't lie to myself. I wasn't happy, and I had to step off the treadmill."

He paused, then continued. "I thought about suicide for a long time. I wanted to die but killing myself was too overwhelming, so I killed my wife to get out of my life. I thought jail would be a kind of death. I don't know where these ideas came from, but they coursed through my head every day, like a TV mystery. One day I got the idea to kill her. I made a plan and I executed it. I was cool and calm and determined to do the job." He stopped, then asked me, "How is it possible, Cuong, that I murdered my own wife in cold blood, without any feeling?"

I said without thinking, "You were unhappy."

When he heard my words, Fred burst into tears. "The worst thing is I didn't know I was suffering. We never spoke about happiness or suffering in my church. Not believing and not being happy were taboo subjects. For the first time, practicing meditation here in prison, I discovered happiness."

I looked at him carefully and said, "Fred, you've always been happy. You just haven't known how to access it. I'm so sorry no one was able to help you. If you'd known the joy within you, you would never have committed that murder."

Fred was crying. "You're right, I wouldn't have. At that point, life was worth nothing to me. I did what I felt I had to to escape my suffering."

"It's not too late," I said.

He looked at me. "I committed murder and went to the police to report myself. They didn't believe me. I had to say it twice, 'I killed my wife.' Now you say it's not too late. But she's dead!"

"Your wife is still there," I said, touching his heart. "You still love her, and that means she's still with you. And you're still in her heart. She wants you to be happy."

Fred cried again. "She loved me. Of course, she'd want me to be happy."

"If you're happy, she'll be happy too. It's not too late."

21.

It's sad that people in the West think Buddhists are nonbelievers. Reverend Fred often came to talk to me about Christianity. My words confused him, but then I'd explain what I meant. One time I told him, "As long as you try to find God within the paradigm of existence and nonexistence, you'll never find Him. Jesus understood this."

In my mind's eye, I saw Fred as free from these either-or concepts, and I saw him as happy and close to God. Fred asked if I'm a believer, and I said, "I am," adding, "a Buddhist believer. When you were a minister, you were a nonbeliever. Now you're a true Christian and a real pastor. Practicing Buddhism deeply, you've touched the depths of your own religion."

"It's crazy, but I feel more religious than ever," Fred said.

What does it mean to be a Buddhist? A true Buddhist is also a Hindu, Christian, Muslim, and Jew. Touching the depths of Buddhism through sitting meditation, Fred touched his own Christianity. We need to explore our faiths more deeply. Happiness is there.

Fred came to our group meditations regularly. He sat quietly, and in doing so, renewed his faith and reawakened his joy. What he loved most was the silence. One day during a talk, I explained that I wasn't trying to transmit a creed, just the "belief" in one's own experience. "If you ask me what I believe in," I said, "I believe in you. My *faith* awakens something in you. Whatever religion you identify with, you need to believe in yourself."

If I'd used my time to teach relaxation, that would have been help- ful but not transformative. I did my best to touch the heart of each prisoner. In individual meetings, I sat quietly and observed my breathing—mindfulness of breathing. But Buddhism is more than mindfulness alone. Buddhism is about insight, helping each person transcend the illusion of separation. The heart of Buddhism is the insight that there's no "I." If a prisoner is attached to an illusory "I," he'll be stuck in despair. If he can get out of the illusion of "I," he'll touch the spaciousness in himself and renew his belief in life. In many initial interviews of just twenty minutes, I was able to help prisoners connect with the profound joy that resides in all of us.

2 2 .

Mike was just nineteen and out of control when he strangled his girlfriend. After the murder, he heard her screaming every night. Sleeping was no longer possible for him. In prison, he wouldn't allow the health service to help him; he just sat alone in his cell, confused and deeply ashamed. The health service referred Mike to me, hoping I could do something.

Mike sat in front of me, his head bent low. I asked if he wanted to sit in silence and suggested he sit up straight so his breathing would be easier. He followed my suggestion, and as we sat together, I felt the depth of his suffering. When we're in silence, we can experience the pain and suffering of others. *Compassion* means "suffering with." We feel the suffering of others.

Mike was stuck in his suffering. I didn't say anything and continued to follow my breathing. After twenty minutes, I experienced a shift in me, my suffering decreased. That was a good sign. I asked Mike if he felt a little better, and he answered softly, "Yes." Now he felt enough peace to talk to me. It was as if he was relearning to speak.

Mike said he didn't know why he killed his girlfriend. She was She was watching TV, and he thought, "I'm going to strangle her." He walked past her and the idea changed. Then he walked behind her a second time, and the idea returned. Again he changed his mind, but the third time he walked past her, he did it. He strangled her to death. Then he went to the river and tried to hang himself from a tree. He put a cord around his neck, but he didn't dare jump. He went home and watched TV, then went to bed.

Mike had been lonely most of his life. His parents divorced and often left him with the neighbors. He lied to them, saying one of his parents was home, and then he stayed home by himself, eating all the junk food he could find and binge-watching TV for days on end.

After a few months sitting with our weekly meditation group, he said, "I don't feel lonely anymore. I've had a taste of happiness. I love to cook and have started cooking for my fellow prisoners." The guards were blown away. Mike had become social, talking to other prisoners and helping them when he could. He had touched hope for the first time in his life.

Once he said to me, "I'm happier now than I've ever been. I found happiness in prison. That's nuts. I'll do what I can to stay happy after I leave here, too."

In Holland, people are given a second chance, and Mike would be able to leave prison after serving his time. You might think he should suffer, he earned this punishment for what he did and doesn't have the right to be happy. Young men like Mike cause a lot of damage to themselves and society because of their suffering. But punishment doesn't help them or society. They need guidance and support so they stop harming themselves and others. Guidance costs less than punishment and lessens recidivism.

How often we miss the chance to help men like Mike, because as a society we have strong ideas about retributive justice—punishment. Every prisoner represents an opportunity to help, which can be redemptive for them and for society as well. Often, it's not difficult to help a prisoner. Many are ripe for the lessons they need. We all make mistakes and have the right to be supported so we can learn new ways of being.

Under my supervision, Mike was able to see his family. In the visitor area, his parents were sitting next to each other. At first, Mike's legs were trembling, but gradually he became calmer. It was an important step for him to be able to accept himself. Family is an important part of everyone's development. The harshest punishment for many prisoners is not being able to see their family members. Sitting with his mom and dad gave Mike an important message: "We will not let you down again." Family is a part of a person's roots, and without roots, we can't be happy. As a Vietnamese man, I know how important it is in my culture never to let a family member down in a difficult situation.

Can we transform our prisons into places of redemption and happiness? I believe we can—if we help prisoners restore their relationships with family, friends, and most of all, themselves. Many prisoners reject their families and friends. Or perhaps they were abandoned or betrayed. They have to rebuild their trust, and we can help them do this.

23.

Mike had become noticeably happier. His sister began visiting him, and he was studying to start a business after his release. He was chosen to be the cleaner of his unit, a job that prisoners like because it gives them more freedom of movement and a slightly higher salary. Each time I spoke with him, I was aware of how painful his past had been and how happy he was now. What if prisons became happy places? Would crime increase or decrease? Most people want a place that scares prisoners from committing crimes again. I think this is a fallacy, since people who aren't happy, who have nothing to lose, are the most dangerous.

In an ideal prison, the day would start with sitting together. Sitting has a positive effect on our lives; we sleep and eat better. During the night, many prisoners come face-to-face with their suffering, recalling what they've done to others. Throughout the day, they might talk and laugh, but at night, they have to feel their painful feelings. Many scream and pound cell doors. The solution in prisons is sleeping pills, but medication doesn't touch the causes of their insomnia. Even with pills, they sleep little and feel their pain.

I advise prisoners to meditate before going to bed, and many who sit quietly for twenty to thirty minutes sleep much better. Mike no longer hears his girlfriend screaming. His deep remorse won't disappear. Regret in itself isn't the problem. If Mike can feel the pain and accept his actions, he can feel whole within. Honesty breeds happiness. Honesty and self-respect are ballasts as we navigate the sea of suffering.

24.

I met many successful people in prison. Hans is one. He was about fifty when he came to our meditation group, and at the end of the session, he told me, out of the blue, "Cuong, I've never been angry in my life." He said it with a lot of pride.

I said, "I don't think that's true. I think you've just never seen your anger."

He was shocked, then burst into tears. I let him cry, and the other prisoners also stayed quiet. Hans had been CEO of a large family business, the only officer who wasn't a member of the family. He was talented and highly appreciated. Everything seemed to be going well in his life. He was calm in all circumstances.

Then one day he came home and began beating his girlfriend. She screamed and cried as he chased her around the house, continuing to hurt her. It went on for about ten minutes.

"Why are you doing this?" she asked, and he had no idea. He went to the police station and told them, "I almost killed my girlfriend."

"I still don't know why I did it," he told me. I instructed him to meditate and observe himself, to look for his anger. He refused to believe he had any anger.

At the end of one meditation session, he spontaneously hugged a fellow prisoner and cried on his shoulder. Three weeks later, I saw him, and he looked really happy. "I've touched my anger," he reported. It was a great discovery for him. Seeing his anger, he saw a part of his life he hadn't allowed himself to know, and suddenly he radiated happiness. He helped his fellow prisoners, taught reading to the ones who couldn't read, and shared his advice for life. It was beautiful to see.

He told me, "I worked hard for thirty years building my life, my house, my family, my career. Then I lost everything. Seeing my anger, I discovered there's more to me than I realized. Although I've lost everything, I found myself. After prison, no one will hire me because I have a record. Maybe I'll have to clean bathrooms or something. But I feel happy. It doesn't mean I won't suffer. But now I can see my suffering. Things went crazy because I couldn't see it. I couldn't see my anger. Maybe I'm naïve, but it feels like nothing can go wrong now. I've seen my suffering and found a profound happiness."

25.

We think people in prison are different from us, that they're "criminals" and we're not. But we're all essentially the same. And some people in jail are innocent, convicted of a crime they didn't commit. That's how I got to know Rick, a neurologist. Three years after he was imprisoned, his innocence was proven. But during those three long years, everything dear to him was broken—his family, his job, his friends, his reputation, his possessions. When I met him, he was angry. He spoke constantly about his innocence.

Few prisoners admit that they're guilty, but some are genuinely innocent.

When I listened to Rick, I believed him. Somehow I knew he was innocent. I understood his anger, experienced his pain, and felt his frustration. In my job, I'm not allowed to take sides, only to accompany each prisoner on his spiritual journey. I told him, "I can help you to be at peace with your situation." That was the beginning of his transformation.

After each meditation session, he was more peaceful than the week before, and when he was retried, he was seen by the court as a man of peace. The judge gave him a literal pat on the back after the hearing. He's not permitted to do that, but he did it spontaneously. His lawyer was surprised, but Rick understood. It was the fruit of practicing meditation, it came from his peace. The judge could feel his innocence.

2 6 .

Being a chaplain was a joy for me, even though I saw a lot of suffering. That kind of negative energy enters your body and mind. Many of my colleagues couldn't stand it and asked for my help finding happiness in their work.

How can we experience happiness in life? It's often thought that Buddhism offers exercises that help you relax and solve problems. This is the way the Buddha's four truths are generally taught. According to this understanding, the first truth is suffering; the second is that suffering has a cause; the third is the possibility of removing the cause of suffering; and the fourth offers eight steps to do this.

Suffering is seen as a problem, and so the cause of the problem must be addressed. To me, the first truth of Buddhism isn't suffering per se, but *suffering as a truth*. At a glance, these might not seem different, but they are. The problem with suffering is when we can't see it. When we can, touching our suffering can be liberating. When Hans, for example, saw the reality of his anger, it was freeing.

The Buddha didn't say suffering, *dukkha*, is a problem to be solved or eliminated. He said it's something to be seen. Nothing is more dangerous than invisible suffering. This is a huge problem in prisons, because suffering there is seen as a weakness.

The second truth in Buddhism is not about problem-solving, unearthing and removing the cause of suffering. The literal meaning is suffering arises, *dukkha samudaya*. *Samudaya* means both origin and arising. Suffering not only arises, it also dies, *dukkha nirodha*, which is the third truth. It doesn't last forever. It remains as long as it's not seen and held onto. Suffering arises and goes away. Removing suffering is a superficial translation. Suffering doesn't need to be removed. It only has to be seen. Buddhism is about understanding, not about getting rid of anything, even suffering.

The extinction of suffering is the extinction of discrimination. Buddhism is not a battle. Discernment, not discriminating, is the basis of Buddhist insight. Doing nothing, just being as fully present as we can, is the fourth noble truth. I have done my best to apply this in prisons, and it helped bring about miracles.

27.

Finn was a muscular man who had a big mouth. He was a fighter and he said whatever he thought. He always entered the meditation hall making a lot of noise—chattering, shouting, and expressing his anger toward everyone. When he joined our group, he was marked "red." In the prisons where I worked, they had a red, orange, and green system. Someone categorized as red was given less freedom of movement.

Finn's anger always lessened during meditation, and he would leave with a smile. The contrast between his arrival and departure was pronounced. Before he learned to meditate, the staff in the prison did everything they could to calm him down, but nothing seemed to work. After just three weeks practicing with our group, the impossible happened. No one could believe it.

I gave Finn a lot of suggestions. "You can't pour tea into a cup that's already full." Then I emptied the cup in front of me and said, "Now there's room. When you're filled with rage, you can't let anything else in. You get mad at the slightest provocation and have little happiness or freedom." That image touched him, and he never forgot it. From that moment on, he began to empty his cup every day.

One day, he told me, "I was attacked in the work hall. It was chickenshit. If you want to hit somebody, don't do it from behind. I fell, stood up, and grabbed the motherfucker by the chest. I could have killed him, but I thought of you. I remembered the teacup and let him go. You saved his life—and mine—Cuong. If I had killed that boy, I would have gotten life, and it's not worth it. I think he was hired to hit me. I couldn't believe I let him go."

I was proud of him. I knew he had changed, but I didn't know he'd be able to calm himself that quickly. After each meditation period, he said, "Empty the cup. Let it go," and after that he was calm and happy.

A week later he said, "I was attacked again, this time by a teenager. He was also hired by someone. He hit me from behind, and again I fell and stood up. I grabbed the boy by the chest, seriously thought about killing him, and once again I let him go. I was strong and confident when I let him go. I feel so free. My wife was happy to hear about it. I'm being transferred to another prison. I'm no longer safe here."

Finn applied the teachings of the Buddha beautifully. The fourth truth is the way to end suffering, *dukkha nirodha marga*. He understood right view, the first practice of the eightfold path. With right view, he did "nothing" in a beautiful way and saved two lives.

2 8 .

The Buddhist path has eight folds: (1) right view, (2) right thinking, (3) right speech, (4) right action, (5) right livelihood, (6) right effort, (7) right attention, and (8) right concentration. This is a foundational teaching. The path begins with the right view. Mindfulness, or right attention, needs wisdom to free us from erroneous ideas and assist us in perceiving the truth of suffering. Suffering is always extinguished (*nirvana*, or *nirodha*) by non-doing. I've seen nirvana in prisoners. Nirvana was the foundation of Finn's success, the liberating happiness that transcends all other happiness.

I call the first truth happiness, *sukha satya*. True happiness is independent of ideas, even ideas of happiness, and it's not something you can find in the future. It's something you can feel, experience, and appreciate in the present moment—and it's most accessible through non-doing.

29.

Like so many young prisoners I met, Jeff had been a pimp, overseeing more than ten women. He protected them and made a lot of money off their services. He described his work this way: "The clients were looking for happiness, but I couldn't give them real happiness. The girls weren't happy, how could they make others happy? So we created an illusion. I trained the girls to assess their customers. What does he want? What is his idea of happiness? What kind of woman does he want? What does he expect from his ideal woman? I trained the girls to pretend they're that woman. Most men need a sweet wife. So girls learned to act sweet—soft and nice. It's an illusion, but my customers were happy and paid a lot for it. I got rich selling illusions."

"You *are* happy" was always my message for prisoners. It's not easy to say it in prison in a credible way. But to describe the first truth as suffering sounds horrifying. We need new expressions and interpretations.

We want happiness, but we end up suffering. Hans suppressed his anger and thought he was happy with his success, but his suffering erupted and he beat up his girlfriend without even knowing why. He lost his money, his career, and his success, but he was lucky. He discovered happiness in prison. Insight, not suppression, can help us recognize real happiness.

Happiness is a truth. We can touch happiness again and again. What is the source of happiness? It isn't money, fame, sex, food, or sleep. The Buddha called these "the five desires" and said none of them could bring lasting happiness. I met prisoners who knew what it was like to have money, and it didn't bring them happiness. Of course, we need money, but money in itself doesn't guarantee happiness. They had a lot of money and were still unhappy.

Jeff made his fortune selling women and drugs, and he walked around with cash in his pockets. "Everyone knew I had money on me, so I packed a revolver. But a gun is only a weapon if you're willing to shoot. If someone standing in front of you wants your money, you pull out your gun, and you let them know you're willing to shoot. They'll know right away if it's true, and they'll kill you if you're bluffing. I lived in that world, and it was tense—miserable, actually—all the time.

Happiness as the first truth of Buddhism is the happiness we all already have. We don't have to conjure it or find the right conditions. We just have to be honest and feel the truth that is within.

30.

Frank sought happiness through sex. He gave his wife drugs, and they went to couples clubs together. He watched his wife be gang-banged by ten men, one after another. He regretted letting things go that far, but he couldn't stop it. He was crying when he told me about it. He couldn't forgive himself. He sought extreme sexual experiences to taste happiness, but they ended in lasting pain.

Getting enough sleep is important, but isn't enough in itself to bring real happiness. Too much sleep stems from the same problem as overeating: the lack of happiness. Satisfying the five desires doesn't bring happiness.

The first truth for our era is that you are already happy, *sukha satya*. *Sukha* is happiness and *satya* is truth. Happiness is the truth. You don't have to do anything to be happy. If we believe that the second truth, *samudaya satya*, requires us to find the cause of happiness, we're working toward a goal and thus continue to suffer. Some people feel lost when they retire. But do we need a goal to be happy? Happiness has no cause. *Samudaya* therefore needs to be retranslated as manifestation. Happiness is a truth, and it's manifested all the time.

Real happiness has no cause. As I see it, this is the second truth. Another way to say it is that the cause of happiness is empty; we cannot name a single thing that causes happiness. We cannot grasp anything. The world is mysterious and liberating. We can stop searching. We no longer have to work to achieve happiness. When we understand that happiness has no cause, whatever direction we look, we see only happiness. The conditions for happiness are present.

When most people begin meditation practice, they need a goal, like peace. But prisoners don't need to achieve anything. I simply say, "We'll sit in silence for thirty minutes." We think aimlessness, *apranihita*, is useless, but thirty minutes spent in a so-called useless way, without searching, reaching, or looking for anything, is priceless.

31.

We have a sense of ourselves as separate individuals looking for connection, but the more we try to find the self that wants to connect, the lonelier we feel. Loneliness is a big problem among prisoners. After he was imprisoned, Gerard became despondent. None of his family members visited him. He had been devoted to them his whole life, and he felt betrayed. How can we free ourselves from the despair of loneliness?

There's a Buddhist teaching called *anatman*, selflessness. To search for a self or a goal or success, we need to separate ourselves from the world, of which we're already an integral part. In meditation, we just sit. It isn't easy for prisoners at first, but they manage. Nothing feels more useless than sitting still without knowing why, yet they did what I instructed, which was nothing. Gerard told me, "When I sit this way, I become one with the world." It was a miracle.

We often act in ways we feel are in our self-interest, failing to consider other people or the space around us. Acting in this way influences our speech and all our other actions. Just sitting without a goal helped the prisoners I taught reconnect with life.

Buddhism is not a self-help exercise. If anything, it's a *non-self*-help exercise. The happiness that arises from the awareness of non-self is far more stable than self-improvement. *Non-self*-awareness helps us love others, and that alone frees us from suffering. When love is present, we're already free from suffering.

3 2 .

Jack thought his girlfriend was perfect. He was a sports instructor who gave private lessons. Most of his clients were well-to-do women. He always behaved properly and professionally, and as his work succeeded, his confidence grew. One day his girlfriend told him how much she hated women who were unfaithful to their partners. It made him feel he could trust her, and he was glad to have such a loyal woman as his partner.

Then seemingly out of the blue, she confessed she was having an affair with his best friend. He asked why, and she said, "You're always away. You never have time for me and I get lonely." Jack felt vertiginous and, as far as he can remember, blacked out. Later he learned he had stabbed her to death.

Everything seemed to be going so well. He had the things people want. But he didn't have time—time to be with his girlfriend, time to listen to her. Love needs nourishing. For his girlfriend, loneliness was a form of starvation. All his energy was wrapped up in his career, and it blinded him. He didn't see what was going on with his best friend. Later he realized he could have known, the signs were there, but he wasn't paying attention.

Even while serving time in prison, Jack continued running after success. He attended classes, worked out at the gym, earned diplomas and certificates. Practicing meditation gave Jack a chance to push the pause button. Slowing the quest for success gave him much-needed time and space. During meditation, he dared to sit still and experience goallessness. He was useless in those moments, and it felt fine. His drivenness ceased, and he began to see his life clearly.

He remembered seeing a condom in his girlfriend's purse, and he asked her why it was there. She said she got it from a man who distributes condoms on the street. Looking back, he saw that was a strange response, but he'd been busy and hadn't given it further thought. He told me, "I could have seen her loneliness, her suffering, and her dishonesty. I didn't realize I had abandoned her by being so busy.

We can stop chasing success. The third truth, *nirvana*, is the extinguishing even of happiness. We no longer run after it. We sit without a goal. We can never experience this happiness unless we take some time to be purposeless. We pursue what we think will bring us happiness, but if we knew that happiness has no cause, we'd stop running. We'd sit still for twenty or thirty minutes, and let this unsettling feeling of uselessness give us clarity. Usually our clarity is covered over by our desires. When we dare to sit still, clarity—and charity—is there.

Pride and a kind of one-pointed stubbornness kept Jack from feeling his pain. He was under the spell of success, and it continued in prison. Only when he sat still did he touch his pain and the pain of his girlfriend and, for the first time, he could cry and feel the depth of his regret. Sitting showed him things he'd never allowed himself to see or feel before. He began to eat and sleep better and feel alive again. This practice of uselessness turned out to be useful.

Meditation helps create a space so we can see what's already there. When we stop our search for happiness, we discover a deeper happiness. It's already in us.

Many prisoners discover through meditation that what they thought would bring them happiness was, instead, delusory. We fabricate the causes of happiness and miss real opportunities to be happy. The third truth is the end of running after happiness and away from suffering. We think happiness is the opposite of suffering, and we strive for something that takes us away from ourselves and our own natural joy.

33.

Buddhist psychology, *Abhidharma*, says that for happiness and suffering to arise, four conditions are needed: the causal-condition, *hetupratyaya*; the support-condition, *adhipatip-ratyaya*; the continuity-condition, *samanantarapratyaya*; and the object-condition, *alambanapratyaya*. Bear with me, I know this sounds complicated.

- The causal-condition, *hetupratyaya*. We suffer because we believe that an object has a prime cause. This is a fabrication of our mind. There is no single cause; effects are the result of multiple causes and conditions. First, we invent a cause, and then we suffer because we believe it's true. The third truth of Buddhism, traditionally called the cessation of suffering—I call it the presence of happiness—puts an end to linear thinking and teaches instead that the idea of a single cause exists only in the mind. All "causes" of happiness exist only in the mind as well. Genuine happiness doesn't need a cause and certainly not a single cause. It's *not conditional*.

- The support-condition, *adhipatipratyaya*, makes it clear that all suffering arises within ourselves. We feed our suffering and also our happiness. A plant needs a seed (causal-condition) to germinate. After that, it needs support elements to grow: rain, sunlight, earth, air, and so on. Suffering is neither natural nor inevitable. It's the result of being fed. We feed our ideas about happiness, and we feed our ideas about suffering. When we stop chasing ideas, we stop suffering. Nirvana is a form of happiness that needs no cause, no food. We don't have to do anything to enjoy nirvana.

Meditating without a goal can help us reach nirvana. When we stop hunting for happiness, we put an end to suffering.

- The continuity-condition, *samanantarapratyaya*, means that suffering needs continuity to exist. When we stop feeding our suffering, discontinuity arises, food ceases, and suffering stops.

- The object-condition, *alambanapratyaya*. Suffering requires an object. We believe someone or something is responsible for our suffering. The object doesn't have to be outside, sometimes we see ourselves as the one responsible. Inmates usually blame someone for their suffering, and often it's themselves. As long as we see someone or something as responsible for our suffering, it continues. This idea of a responsible party is a fabrication. When we can see this, anger, hatred, and depression all stop.

When any one of these four conditions is absent, there is nirvana. The flames of suffering are extinguished. Only nirvana can free us from our limited ideas about happiness. Only real happiness can supplant false happiness. When we sit still, we stop feeding our suffering. This is nirvana, and it's life-changing.

3 4 .

Ed was a quiet young man. He didn't say much when we met. Like most of the prisoners I spent time with, he hadn't been well-cared for growing up. I gave him my love and full attention, and watched him begin to feel safe.

Being alone is probably the greatest pain prisoners face. They're separated from family and friends. For most, the sense of separation began long before incarceration. "My mother was a shopaholic," Ed told me. "She bought so much stuff we didn't have space to live." His suffering wasn't about her shopping—it was about loneliness.

Through meditation, Ed touched the impact these experiences had on him. He was able to feel his hatred but also his mother's vulnerability. With my guidance, he wrote his mother a love letter, thanking her for all she'd done for him despite her own pain.

Through our work together, I watched Ed transform from an adolescent to a man. This was possible, in part, because I could already see his maturity. Someone who is mature struggles to find his own ideas and perspectives. To be free and whole, we need to think for ourselves.

When I looked at Ed, I saw his family, his ancestors, the whole society. Ed wasn't in prison because only he had done something wrong. The whole society was, in part, responsible for his actions. We need to use our insight and not just call Ed "Ed." Ed is not alone. He represents all of us.

We're seen and judged as individuals with names. But if we loosen the grip of our name and who we're expected to be, we become pure. Ed's essence is unique and at the same time, a part of something greater. The court found him guilty, but in my heart, I know he is a part of me and of us all. I could only help Ed when I saw this. When I didn't see it, I remained in judgment based on an idea of Ed that was really about my own limitations.

We think we're safe when those we believe are evil are locked up. But there is a criminal in each of us, and if we don't know him or her—like Hans who came home and beat up his girlfriend—then we're not safe. Hans had no idea where that dark emotion came from. Until we understand ourselves, we are prisoners of our loneliness and of our ignorance. Only insight, not locking away parts of ourselves, can make us safe.

35.

After learning about the phenomenon from Reverend Fred, I began to hear the other prison chaplains saying they don't believe— meaning they don't believe in God. When I felt into what they were saying, I think they meant they didn't believe in themselves. There's no difference between believing in God, another person, one of the prisoners, or yourself. It's essential that chaplains believe in prisoners. If they don't, what can they offer? When faith radiates from a person, you can feel it, and it engenders transformation.

We all need people in our lives who don't judge us. Prisoners are surrounded by people with prejudices about them. They need chaplains who are open. Someone who is attached to concepts will radiate discrimination. Right view is the belief in the wholeness of yourself and others. You look at a prisoner, at anyone, and you see the Buddha.

I read an interview with Bettina Stanghneth, a philosopher who thinks it's wrong to understand prisoners. She told an interviewer, "Look at the way we talk about terrorists. We want to understand them. We say things like, 'They kill because they had a bad childhood.' Apparently, criminals can't think clearly, as we do. Apparently, they don't know right from wrong, how bad they actually are."[1]

Dr. Stanghneth assumes that terrorists are "bad," which goes hand-in-hand with the belief that we are "good." Thinking this way can never bring us together. We turn our backs on the bad people and

---

1 Loenie Breebaart, "Denken is het gevaarlijkste instrument dat we hebben," *Dagblad Trouw* (May 4, 2017).

cut off communication. In the same interview, she was asked, "Does understanding a criminal mean you approve of his actions?"

"That's exactly the problem," she answered. "Once you connect understanding to apologies or justification, you stand on the side of the perpetrator ..."

For Stanghneth, there are two sides—the side of the perpetrator and the side of the victim. Prisoners and terrorists are perpetrators, and it's unfair to see them, even for a moment, as victims themselves. It becomes frightening to understand them, as if doing so would condone their actions. To me, understanding is the deepest form of thought. It's no longer based on good and bad. This is what I mean by *belief*. It's a kind of openness, what Zen Master Shunryu Suzuki called "beginner's mind." Unless you have faith in someone, you can't help him, and the only alternative is punishment. Prisoners need help, not punishment.

3 6 .

Right speech always goes with deep listening. Keith spoke to me for an hour, and within that time he was able to tell me about an aunt who abused him, and he began to feel some relief. At the end of our second meeting, he asked what my secret was. I don't have a secret. I listen to inmates the way I listen to myself. People today are distracted, and deep listening is rare. We need to create space in ourselves, without thinking about or doing other things.

Connection starts with posture and breath. Sitting upright and breathing mindfully, we demonstrate that we're there for the other person, that we take them seriously and are listening with respect. Prisoners already feel less than whole, and if you listen inattentively, they won't tell you much. Sitting with a straight back, you show your presence, that you take them and their difficulties seriously, and that's energizing for everyone.

As a meditator, I've been trained to sit straight. When I began Zen practice twenty years ago, I didn't understand why that was important, but during conversations like those in prison, the value was clear. The quality of listening grows directly from the quality of sitting. Even when I heard something horrible, I continued to sit upright, and it helped free me from any judgments.

The Buddha said, "My teaching is good at the beginning, good in the middle, and good at the end." Sitting is the same. We sit upright at the beginning, in the middle, and at the end. We need stability to hear such difficult stories. When a prisoner or anyone who has experienced profound trauma sees us become destabilized, they'll stop talking. Being present with my back upright, I was able to change the atmosphere of the prison.

Sit straight, on your sitz bones (not on your tailbone), your spine upright, your head in line with your shoulders. Sitting straight supports breath, and breathing supports sitting. I always asked prisoners to join me sitting this way, and in my experience, the invitation was appreciated.

37.

Conscious breathing brings body and mind together, and it also brings two people together. When I breathe consciously, I become one with the person I'm speaking with. Doing so, I'm able to experience his feelings shift from pain to peace. The strong belief that we are individuals with firm boundaries is not supported by the reality that we can experience other people's feelings. Are we really individuals, or is this just a concept?

Many young prisoners with ADHD think they can't sit still. But when I sat still, they could too. I sat with them in meditation, and many were able to sit as solidly as a mountain. Breathing together, we experienced connection, and the separation between "self" and "other" dissolved.

As soon as these prisoners connected with me through breathing, their listening was activated. Even before they spoke, we were both in deep listening. I listened first to their feelings—often experiences of pain and depression. I didn't experience it as *their* pain and *their* depression, I felt it as mine. We listen well to others by listening to ourselves. Neuroscience bears this out. Empathic listening blurs the boundary between your feelings and my feelings. To help someone else is to help yourself.

It begins with conscious breathing. Conscious breathing helps us listen to ourselves and thus to others. What are we listening to? Through ourselves, we listen to the prisoner. I always experienced pain when I listened to these men, a hidden, unseen pain that's been denied, usually for a long time. When pain becomes life-threatening, we shift into denial to survive and act as if the pain isn't there. By breathing with each other, the pain is exposed, and the prisoner no longer can hide his pain. I know about it, and now he knows about it, too. Communication is established. After a lifetime of not feeling his own pain, denial is disrupted. Breathing brings back his communication with himself, and that begins to heal the damage.

After the initial discomfort, the prisoners I worked with enjoyed this self-discovery, even enjoyed, in a deep sense, their own pain. They were happy to be with it. It's not easy to go into pain; you need guidance and support. Both the prisoners and I need the courage to lead them toward the pain. Seeing one's own pain is difficult to sustain, but by staying with it, we can witness pain transform into joy. It cannot be otherwise. There's no difference between suffering and happiness, pain and joy. Listening and looking, if done correctly, transforms pain to joy, and the process can be quick. After twenty minutes breathing together, there was joy in both of us. It's beautiful to experience peace after so many years of suffering. Of course, in other cases it can take months or years to tolerate the pain inside us. Regardless of time, the fruit is always a relief, and provides a sense of wholeness.

The Buddha discovered the truth of suffering while listening deeply to his own heart. Where does suffering come from? Suffering has an important place in the lives of prisoners. Most end up incarcerated because of suffering. Not enough attention is paid to the suffering of prisoners. Guards suffer too, and they haven't learned to deal with their suffering either. And they're constantly exposed to suffering. Year after year, this energy enters them, and they get worn out, which in turn affects the prisoners.

38.

Sitting upright and breathing consciously, I was able to feel and hear the prisoners' hearts even before they said anything. If we listen well, we do so without judging. Buddhists call it compassionate listening, represented by the archetypal bodhisattva Avalokiteshvara:

We invoke your name, Avalokiteshvara. We aspire to learn your way of listening in order to help relieve the suffering in the world. You know how to listen in order to understand. We invoke your name in order to practice listening with all our attention and open-heartedness. We will sit and listen without any prejudice. We will sit and listen without judging or reacting. We will sit and listen in order to understand. We will sit and listen so attentively that we will be able to hear what the other person is saying and also what is being left unsaid. We know that just by listening deeply, we already alleviate a great deal of pain and suffering in the other person.[2]

Artful listening allows us to understand and transform suffering, and when we understand suffering, we don't judge anyone. When suffering is invisible, it pushes us around. Deep listening makes the inaudible audible. Most prisoners are not yet strong enough emotionally to listen to their own suffering; they need help. It's while telling their stories to someone who is listening well that many discover their suffering, perhaps for the first time. Facing suffering allows us to taste freedom. It frees us from not knowing what's animating us. A good companion can help a prisoner listen to his own heart. A good companion can give a prisoner confidence that what he has to say is important.

---

2   Thich Nhat Hanh, *Chanting from the Heart: Buddhist Ceremonies and Daily Practices* (Berkeley: Parallax Press, 2002), 33.

Bert couldn't stand to be touched by his mother or sister, or even by his friends. Loving affect was unbearable to him. He felt happiest fighting, and as a result, he often ended up in prison. I listened to him after breathing together. He appreciated our conversations and promised he would continue mindful breathing in his cell. He sat in meditation every day, and one day he made a great discovery: He remembered having been abused by his uncle. It was a breakthrough; at last he saw the source of his suffering.

When he was little, he was often showered by his uncle. His uncle fondled him while drying his body. It aroused strange feelings in him. He didn't understand the feelings, but knew after that he didn't want to be hugged by anyone, not even his mother or sister. He didn't understand what was going on, and he kept it to himself. Later in life, he was unable to express love.

Meditating in his cell, he discovered why he was so shut down, and after that he began to soften. When his mother came to visit, he told her about his discovery, and she told him she'd been abused by the same man, her own brother. For the first time in as long as he could remember, he was able to hug his mother. They both cried. He was free of his ignorance. The cause of his suffering was not only the abuse, but also not understanding what was inhibiting his behavior.

Freed from not knowing, Bert became really happy. After he was released from prison, he got a job, regained his self-esteem, and became close with his sister for the first time. She cried. "I've waited so long. I love you very much and didn't understand why you wouldn't let me touch you. I love how soft you are now, like a child."

Listening can work wonders. It's less costly and more effective than punishment. Listening deeply, we create a world with happier people in it.

39.

Quality listening has four dimensions: posture, breathing, attention, and silence. The first three take practice. The fourth—being quiet—only requires "doing nothing." I begin all my conversations with prisoners with an invitation to sit quietly together. When our thinking is quieted, even for a few moments, the door to silence opens up, and in that silence we can feel our pain.

We make sense of ourselves and the world through patterns of thought. When these habits of thinking and observing stop, we touch another dimension—silence, where misunderstanding is extinguished and clarity arises. Touching silence can change a person's life in a matter of moments.

In my experience, all prisoners enjoyed silence. They came to meditation to sit quietly together, free from imprisonment for an hour. In those moments, they felt truly alive, the hopelessness inside soothed. Most prisoners think life will resume only after they're released. They're always living in the future. But in the depth of that silence, they discovered new life and experienced happiness. Silence is a scarce and precious resource, especially in a prison. Time and time again, I saw how a few minutes of quiet sitting can bring forth profound happiness.

When prisoners gather with someone quiet, they can enjoy quiet. If you start a conversation on a foundation of silence, the other person will join you in that deep, quiet space. Touching this peace, transformation becomes possible. There are many relaxation techniques, but few lead to the depths of real silence. These techniques can free you from difficulties by avoiding or suppressing them, but the difficulties always return, and sometimes return stronger. In silence, we see things as they are, and this insight cannot be taken from us. After a while, the prisoners fell silent as soon as they arrived at the meditation hall, and I watched the silence grow in them as they got stronger and more stable.

After one meditation session, I held up a Buddha statue and asked, "Who is this?"

They looked up and said, "It's the Buddha."

I said, "Try again," and waited. When there was no follow-up response, I said, "It's you. It's a selfie!" Then I handed each of them a statue of the Buddha to keep in their cell. I felt it would remind them of the dimension of peace and quiet. We don't have to *do* anything to touch that dimension. We just have to sit still, be quiet, and do nothing.

40.

Buddhism distinguishes between happiness with desire and happiness without desire. The former isn't real happiness. We always want more and can never get enough. The Buddha compared this state to a dog gnawing on a bone with no meat. Gnawing will never satisfy its hunger. In our prison meditation group, the men encountered *happiness without desire* for the first time. When you touch that feeling, you stop searching; you know real happiness. Listening to others helps them experience this kind of happiness and becomes a new guidepost for them.

Many prisoners are prone to depression. They need a different kind of energy to move forward. I don't view depression as a disease. According to Buddhism, depression is a taste of the first truth, the existence of suffering. Suffering is a truth, not a disease. It's a reality that must be seen and felt. Suffering is dangerous only when it's not known. When we suffer from depression, there is pain we don't want to feel, pain we haven't learned to face. We think we can't face it, that we're not strong enough. But we underestimate ourselves.

We think depression is a personal problem, but it's also a social problem. Many prisoners are loners, lonely people who suffer. This sense of self leads to depression. How can we let prisoners know they're not alone? Many of their families have let them down. No one visits them, thinks, or cares about them. It's not surprising they feel depressed. The horizontal connection has been broken, and so they need a vertical connection. That connection is brought about by silence, the source of true happiness. Healing depression starts with connection. I've seen people with depression sit with someone whose vertical connection is intact, and they walk away free from depression, at least temporarily, in a matter of minutes.

41.

When Raid came home after being released from prison, his wife didn't recognize him. He spoke to her and their children in an entirely new way—with love, *maitri*. During his time in prison, Raid had connected with love and happiness within himself, and he took the fruits of his insight home.

Happiness is more than a nice feeling or a positive outlook. Once the good feeling is gone, we'll be angry and dissatisfied again. When we cultivate real happiness, we know how to deal with difficulties that arise after the pleasant feelings pass. Ex-cons often experience challenging external circumstances. Things don't go well financially; there isn't enough money for the family to make ends meet. Sometimes things don't go well in relationships; their wives or partners go out with someone else while they're serving time. That happened to Mark. He was having difficulty reaching his wife, and at one point I said, "I think she's with someone else."

He laughed nervously. I explained why I thought so, but he couldn't believe it. "She wouldn't do that," he told me. A month later, he learned it was true. "How did you know," he asked, then added, "Your words helped me when I got the news. At least I wasn't totally surprised. Still, I'm really pissed. Will I ever be happy again, Cuong?"

It was a good question. At the moment, being happy again seemed impossible. He couldn't sleep and was angry with everyone. I taught him about *maitri*, the first aspect of true love, the capacity we each have to be happy. He didn't understand. "How can I possibly be happy knowing that my wife is sleeping with another man—in my bed?"

I said, "Don't underestimate yourself. You think you can be happy only under certain conditions."

Mark and I sat together, and suddenly he touched a happiness that was still there. He was surprised. "How is it possible? I'm in pain and I feel happy at the same time."

Being happy when everything is going well isn't real happiness. Mark had a beautiful wife and two lovely children. He had a good salary; everything was going well until he landed in jail for transporting drugs. It was a painful journey for him. Prisoners usually think they'll only be happy when they're free again. But after their release, many are still desperate because they no longer have a stable base outside. In their hopelessness, they become unhappy, even dangerous and capable of committing murder or suicide. Learning to practice *maitri*, unconditional love and happiness, is essential for anyone reentering society.

Mark became obsessed with the idea of killing his wife. It took work, but gradually, as he found happiness even while still in pain, he let go of that idea. He said, "I'm no longer afraid of life. I've experienced the worst; things can only get better now. If I can be happy now, I can be happy anytime." He played sports in prison and made a lot of friends on the inside. I saw him regularly, and he asked me again, "How did you know she was with someone else?"

I told him, "Your wife was in a lot of pain and desperate to be with someone." I told him that she hurt as much as he did, and asked him to think about what he might do now to alleviate her pain. He said she had to alleviate *his* pain. "I'm the one in prison."

I reminded him, "You've discovered happiness. She hasn't."

He knew it was true. He was in pain, but he had also tasted true happiness. His wife hadn't. For the first time since discovering that his wife was with someone else, he allowed himself to feel her pain and suffering, and at a certain point was able to say, "I won't kill her. I won't see her again, but I won't hurt her. You helped me taste happiness, and now you've shown me my wife's pain. I feel sorry for her."

Maitri is our capacity to be happy. *Karuna*, another kind of love, is our ability to reduce suffering. They work together. Happiness is only real when it reduces suffering. Often when we think we're happy, it's not the kind of happiness that releases pain. Only true happiness can do that. As a pimp, Peter enjoyed money and luxuries and he thought he was happy. He discovered the truth when he saw the emaciated and addicted girl who worked for him. When her suffering became clear to him, he realized he wasn't happy either. How could anyone be happy while making another suffer that way?

42.

Many prisoners feel the harm they've done only after they discover happiness within themselves. Happiness arises when we feel our suffering; denying suffering makes it (and us) harder.

Meditation creates space, allowing repressed suffering into consciousness. Through silent sitting, we discover a deep happiness that's already there, and which allows room for our suffering. *Karuna* is the capacity to see and respect both our own suffering and the suffering of others. If we don't feed our suffering, it will diminish. We know what suffering is, we recognize it, and we don't feed it. We do nothing to strengthen it. The moment Mark saw his wife's suffering, he stopped blaming her, which reduced his suffering as well.

Maitri gets stabilized with *karuna*. In Vietnamese, we say *maitri-karuna (từ bi)*. Joining *maitri* with *karuna* erases the false divide between happiness and suffering. Happiness is not better than suffering. Being able to see suffering actually allows us to be happy. People usually see suffering as negative. Self-help exercises emphasize positivity, seeing suffering as an enemy that must be overcome. We need to be careful. It's important to leave our suffering as it is.

As long as we want to get rid of our suffering, we can't see it. And the more we try to get rid of it, the stronger it becomes. With *karuna*, we reduce suffering by seeing it—that's all—doing nothing with it. Prisoners need help seeing their own suffering. *Maitri* allows us to see happiness and *karuna* to see suffering. Being with our suffering or the suffering of others is a gift. If you can do it, you'll be stronger. By meditating, you'll become stronger and softer, thanks to *maitri-karuna*.

We can help people who have committed criminal offenses by showing them the suffering they've caused. That pierces the armor of not feeling pain—their own or that of others. It's important to feel our resistance, our dissociation, and our armor. The sooner we stop fighting or shutting down, the faster we can be with our pain. Everyone has the ability to see happiness and suffering. Schoolchildren should be encouraged to develop this capacity and use it throughout their lives.

Reducing suffering doesn't mean not feeling pain. We continue to feel our pain; that's what we need. If prisoners feel pain, they won't repeat the same mistakes in the future. When they fight, they're avoiding feeling or seeing the pain. Over time, they become insensitive to it. Punishment alone won't help. Some prisoners become even more inured to pain and suffering because of their prison sentences. They get harder and more willing to be violent. Prisoners need guidance to be able to feel their own pain and the pain they've inflicted on others.

43.

True love, love that makes both parties happy, is called *mudita* in Buddhism. *Mudita* brings joy, laughter, and satisfaction; we're content with life.

Prisoners are often dissatisfied with a lot of things, including the food they're served. In Dutch prisons, they get a plastic box of food every day to heat up in a microwave. Prisoners have told me it's tasteless and has zero nutritional value.

When we learn to meditate, food tastes better. Gilbert was skeptical, but willing to try. I taught him eating meditation and advised that he turn off the TV while eating. Some prisoners have televisions on twenty-four hours a day, even while they're asleep. The TV gives them comfort, the feeling of contact with life. I think it's the opposite. To me, TV ensures they have no contact with their own feelings, and thus no connection with life.

Gilbert enjoyed eating without the TV. In itself that was an important change. He focused on his dinner instead. Before eating, he practiced conscious breathing, then mindful eating while sitting up straight. It was a ceremony, and he was surprised to find that he liked it.

If we don't appreciate what we have, we might destroy it. Prisoners think about what they don't have and forget what they do. Most still have their health. Prisoners work hard to stay healthy; they do a lot of physical exercise. And now they have some spiritual exercises. Through breathing, they return to themselves and begin to appreciate what they have. They have food. Gilbert sat and looked at his food box and slowly took a bite. I had suggested he chew thirty times before swallowing. He did it and found the food did have some taste. I believe he tasted the food, and also life. He tasted satisfaction, and his life began to change. He became quieter and more appreciative of life. Prisoners often think they'll be happy only when they're released. If they're dissatisfied now, I think they'll be dissatisfied when they're released, too.

We can always find some satisfaction in our lives. It's possible to fall in love with life. This love is only possible with satisfaction. When we're dissatisfied, we don't recognize our suffering or know happiness. By encouraging someone to be satisfied with what he has, we help him discover peace.

Gilbert took twenty minutes to eat his meal. Till then, he'd never taken more than five. I taught eating meditation to the whole meditation group, and many found that the food tasted better. Food is important for prisoners, but mindful eating is an art they hadn't imagined. They usually ate with anxiety. We underestimate the power of eating well. I asked them to do eating meditation at least one meal a day. Some made it a habit and practiced at every meal. After his first taste of eating meditation, Gilbert stopped throwing away his food box.

With *mudita*, we're satisfied with what we have and how we are. When we're not satisfied, it affects our sleep. Some of the detainees who came to our group through health referrals had sleep disorders. Meditating for ten minutes before bed helped them sleep better. During that time, they were present—and still—with their pain. They were there for themselves and content with everything, receiving both happiness and pain equally, and with a deep kind of satisfaction.

I wasn't happy to hear them say things like, "Once a crook, always a crook." A prison therapist told one man he would be an addict for the rest of his life. I see it differently. Prisoners can carve out moments when they're free from anger or addiction. It's a thought. You believe you are a crook, you believe you are an addict, and you act accordingly. You need guidance to touch your Buddha nature. When I see a prisoner, I see the Buddha. Acting in an evil way doesn't mean Buddha-hood isn't possible. Seeing the Buddha in a prisoner is important, it is a moment of *upeksha*, equanimity, in which *there's no difference between a crook and a Buddha*. This is a beautiful teaching in Buddhism.

As Buddhas, prisoners have deep insights we can rely on. They have the power and wisdom to resolve difficult situations. Most guidance given in prison assumes the prisoners need to learn from the supervisors. I think it's the other way around. I've learned a lot from prisoners. They've been through hell, and I have faith in their wisdom. Recognizing this changes the way I listen to them.

When you have confidence in someone's wisdom, you listen without interpreting. You don't have to filter out what's not important. Preconceptions form an image of reality, but they're *not* reality, just interpretations, and they can be inaccurate. Our image of the other has nothing to do with reality. It's a mirror for us. When we can see the other, we see the Buddha.

4 4 .

The Buddhist teaching of *anatman* means "no self." With no "I" or I-image, we're free of comparisons and judgments, such as I'm better (or worse) than you. In either case, we don't see the other. If we're not free of an I-image, we can't listen. Having an I-image hinders love. To live with equanimity, or *upeksha*, requires both wisdom and love.

A chaplain or spiritual counselor needs humility. Knowledge can be a hindrance. Preaching is not the most effective way to help prisoners. Silence can be a powerful means of communication. I prefer questions to answers. Questions offer space and respect. If we see a prisoner as a Buddha, we'll experience the Buddha in that prisoner.

To see the Buddha in a prisoner, a chaplain must free himself of the idea that this person is a criminal. I saw a video in which a chaplain was guiding a prisoner to be aware of his breath and—without judging—of his body, feelings, and thoughts. The chaplain said, "That's all you need." I don't think so. We need more than to look without judgment. We need to see the Buddha in each other. Without the Buddha, mindfulness is incomplete. The Buddha's presence deepens everything.

45.

To speak, we need to listen with respect, admiration, and attention. To listen, we need love. We can speak from the heart only when we listen from the heart. Right speech touches the other person's heart and increases their self-confidence. Words are magical. If we see something beautiful in another person, we can tell them.

Right view helps us see the beauty in others, and we can say aloud what we've discovered. When I'm with a prisoner, I always discover hidden jewels. An hour just flies by. If the good I see in him is based on right view, it can release a lot of strength and energy. A few words of appreciation can change a person's life.

The contact that prisoners have with life on the outside is often filled with arguments—not listening to each other and talking about horrible things. I asked prisoners to meditate for ten minutes before making a phone call, and because of this, Jed resolved a big problem with his girl-friend. He was anxious when she didn't answer the phone right away, and his anxiety leaked into their conversation. "I need her to tell me the truth. If she doesn't want me anymore, I need her to tell me. I hate lies," he told me.

His anxiety affected his girlfriend, and she stopped picking up the phone. When he started meditating before making calls, he touched peace within himself and left anxiety-free messages. His girlfriend started picking up again, and she told him, "I have a boy-friend." It was painful to hear, but he was glad to know the truth, thanks to his right speech.

46.

When prisoners help each other, they usually think, "What's in it for me? What can I get out of it?" After meditating, some of them began to be present for each other without an ulterior motive. When Hans came to prison after a successful business career, he felt he didn't belong "among these petty thieves." Eventually, he admitted how lonely he was, and he made his peace being "among thieves." It was transformative, and he reached out to his fellow prisoners and taught those who couldn't read or write. He found a home, and peace, in prison.

When we are lonely, we have no home. Many prisoners feel this way. Helping one another is a wonderful way to find a home while still in prison. I often asked prisoners to help each other, and those who did, benefited. Some contacted other former inmates after they got out, sharing the happiness they'd discovered through meditation. If you can't share happiness, it's not real happiness.

Many younger prisoners accepted Hans' help writing letters. Later, one man asked him how to start a business, and he offered advice without asking for anything back. That is right action based on unconditional love. It's the way out of loneliness. Surrounded by men who came to love him, Hans was no longer lonely. Giving without asking for anything in return is pure generosity. Generosity is the antidote to stealing.

Grandpa Manuel had trouble sleeping. He saw ghosts and heard strange noises. But he was there for others and asked his wife to help former inmates too. After years of being a refugee in his heart, Manuel was no longer lonely, and in this sense, he was no longer "in prison." He was already free, surrounded by fellow prisoners who loved him. Right action is important while you are behind bars. It prepares you for re-entry into society.

Helping people come back to life is an antidote to killing. I met prisoners who were, for all intents and purposes, dead. Hopeless and without purpose, they'd given up on life. When we see someone who has lost the will to live, if we don't help, we commit a kind of murder. After Grandpa Manuel came back to life, he brought many others with him.

Helping is a source of satisfaction. When you're happy, you're stable. Prison knocks you off balance. You lose your family and friends. Many are imprisoned at a young age and grow up without intimate connections. Throwing someone off-balance influences his sexual behavior. Only when we're in balance is our sexual life in balance too.

47.

Some prisoners are close with their families. If we lock up someone like this, we can't ignore how their families will fare. We need both to create a healthy environment inside and to support prisoners' families. More than a few of the men I counseled had a parent in prison while they were growing up. Many of these men were, in some ways, children themselves.

While teaching an introductory class on Buddhism, I told the prisoners that during their time inside, they had plenty of time for the assignments I gave them. One young man corrected me: "We need time to take care of our families. It takes us longer because we have to arrange everything by phone. And we need time to talk to our kids, who are suffering because we're not there." Until then, I had thought of prisoners as separate from their families, but it's not true. The moment we put someone in prison, we impact his family, including his children. It's sad that prisons make it so expensive for inmates to use the payphones, even to call home.

In each prisoner, I also saw an innocent child. Prisoners return to a childhood innocence. Everything is provided for them, and they can laugh and cry and, with a lot of imagination, relive their childhoods. But many are addicted to drugs so they don't have to feel their pain. Using, they ignore themselves, their pain, and their families, which keeps them on the wheel of suffering. Meditation can help them get back to themselves, their pain, and their families.

I explained that when things go well for them, their families feel it. In the culture I was brought up in, there's no distinction between a person and his family.

4 8 .

Upon release, many prisoners go home empty-handed and have to resume supporting their families. Some are deeply wounded and can barely function. Why should they be left on their own to solve these problems? If we don't help them, the likelihood things will go wrong again is high. We punish them and then take little responsibility for their support and rehabilitation.

We think in numbers. Happiness is expressed in money. If you're rich, you're happy. One prisoner I taught had a lot of money and felt that nothing could go wrong when he got out. He believed the money would provide for his happiness, but that was an illusion. Wealth alone does not bring happiness.

In Buddhism, generosity is a measure of happiness. Monks were beggars who gave Dharma talks to those who offered them food. This exchange was an economic model in balance. Giving with a pure heart is called *dana*. In modern society, we don't know much about giving, just taking. A healthy economy requires balance, a fair exchange. Taking without giving destabilizes individuals and the economy.

Quite a few of the prisoners I met were talented, compassionate, and intelligent. They needed to learn not to run after money but to think deeply about what they could do for society. What did they have to give? We need to give former prisoners a chance to return to society without as much stress. Their time in prison has already alienated them from society. Now they need time to re-enter and to think about how they want to support society.

To allay the anxieties of those in my meditation groups, I told them not to be afraid of unemployment. Everyone has something to give, and if you have something to give, you'll find a place in the world. It might be happiness. The happiness of one person is important. A prisoner or ex-prisoner may not know it yet, but they can give their happiness to society, even through one person. And whatever they do, they can do it with happiness.

The training they receive in prison is preparation for work after their release. If they don't recognize the happiness already in them, things might go wrong again. If their livelihood is based on taking and not giving, their lives will be out of balance again.

A prisoner is a product of his society. Our thinking about economics is out of balance. We want to own as much as possible and give as little as we can. The principle of supply and demand must be transformed into generosity—giving and receiving.

49.

The Dalai Lama has said that "the purpose of life is happiness." We think happiness is what we feel when we get what we want. Economics is based on the pursuit of that kind of happiness. But there's another kind of happiness, happiness that is already there, happiness you don't have to look for. In Buddhism, we call it "giving without giving." A Dharma talk, for example, gives you something you already have. It's the same with *awakening*. You don't wake up due to practicing Buddhism. Awakening is already there. It has no beginning and no end. If it did, it wouldn't be real awakening.

When I see a prisoner, I know he is already awakened, and so I encourage him to sit in silence to discover this for himself. Sitting this way requires faith and trust. I believe in each inmate, that they are already awakened, and I touch something in them that can help transform their suffering. It's not something I do. The awakened state was present before our birth. It's not the result of practice.

The eightfold path starts with right view, or insight. That is the foundation, not mindfulness. Mindfulness is a product of consciousness; understanding helps us be free of consciousness. By consciousness, I mean being stuck in thinking, feeling, suffering, blaming, expecting, worrying, and being afraid. In twenty minutes of sitting quietly, we can step out of all that; this is the power of awakening. As soon as we discover our awakened nature, we discover happiness that has no beginning or end. Real happiness feeds us, and these prisoners were able to feel that.

50.

Buddha means "one who has awakened." Anyone who has awakened is a Buddha. This is the essence of Buddhism.

Practice starts with the assumption that as human beings we need guidance to live with fewer hindrances. Mindfulness practice is scientific; awakening is *insightific*. This isn't a word (yet), but it expresses what I mean. Insight brings us the capacity to believe in ourselves and others. Knowledge is always dualistic. Wisdom is nondual.

Faith arising from duality is conditional. It is not true faith. For example, if you're nice, I believe in you. Real belief is unconditional.

It is not scientific, but insightific. It goes beyond individuality or duality.

Kerry was a house painter who received his wages in cash. When he came home, he gave the money to his wife, and she managed it well. But one day he thought, "Why am I giving it all to her?" When her happiness stopped being enough, things began to go wrong. "I'm in prison because of the decision I made that day," he told me. "It set me on the wrong track."

Science separates people. Insight brings people together. In modern times, we're growing apart without noticing it. We feel lonelier than ever. We look for our own space, our own comfort, our own happiness. Thinking we have to take care of ourselves first before we can think of others is not insightful. In reality, there is no difference between us and others. These boundaries we stick to aren't real. We made them up.

A prisoner asked me, "How do I know I'm on the right path?" It's a good question. We often believe we're on the right path, then one day something goes wrong, but we don't discover it until it's too late. My answer was, "We don't know. We need to ask the Buddha within."

51.

There are three bases of happiness: intelligence, feelings, and connection. We need all three.

Intelligence helps us achieve our goals. But intelligence can be limited when emotions no longer flow unimpeded. If we can't feel our feelings, we cannot be happy. A feeling, pleasant or unpleasant, can be a source of happiness. Happiness is not just having a pleasant feeling. It's also being present with an unpleasant one.

The third form of happiness is stability, or connection. When Mark forgave his ex-wife after she went out with someone else and abandoned him, he found stability.

We can also connect with ourselves and others through our ancestors. There is the horizontal aspect of people we know and the vertical dimension of our ancestors. Connection with our ancestors is stabilizing. We contribute to the stability of each member of our family.

Many prisoners are intelligent, but don't feel their feelings or have a stable base of support. Familial happiness has been disrupted for many prisoners. When you grow up in a family with an alcoholic parent, you can be the victim of abuse. Many prisoners tell stories of alcoholism and violence in their families of origin, and these issues hamper their ability to feel. Later, they may still have a distorted understanding of happiness.

Meditation can help us know deeper forms of happiness. It can help us connect with our feelings and thus, our stability. Numbness is a hindrance that leads to isolation. Feeling our feelings is very important.

Connection is the highest form of happiness. To reenter society successfully, a prisoner needs to know his own feelings. The happiness of connecting with yourself—the pain and the joy—is the surest road home.

5 2 .

Coming home means being happy again. Being able to feel always brings us home, and there is a liberating connection with the whole society. We connect with the visible world, and we also connect with the invisible world.

It is the responsibility of society to bring prisoners home. A prison must be a place where we receive our lost children with open arms.

It must be a place of love. We cannot kill a person if he has behaved badly. We have a responsibility to bring those who are lost home. We can't be happy without everyone; happiness is something we share together.

As a spiritual counselor in four prisons, I saw prisoners who were able to come home, and it was deeply moving to me. Violence in them had been transformed into love and understanding. Sometimes prisoners would sit together quietly and not say much. They simply enjoyed the silence—and not only the silence in the environment, but also the silence in themselves. They knew the value of that silence. Every one of them ended up in prison through noise. If they had known a home in themselves, they would not have been imprisoned. We miss many opportunities to help prisoners, to bring them back home, to reintegrate them into society. They need guidance from people who know where home is. Home is a place of peace and happiness, and it is there for everyone.

About the Author

Cuong Lu, a Buddhist teacher, scholar, and writer, was born in Nha Trang, Vietnam, in 1968 and emigrated to the Netherlands with his family in 1980. He majored in East Asian studies at the University of Leiden, and in 1993 was ordained a monk at Plum Village in France under the guidance of Thich Nhat Hanh. In 2000, he was recognized as a teacher in the Lieu Quan line of the Linji School of Zen Buddhism. During the Lamp Transmission Ceremony, Thich Nhat Hanh offered Cuong this insight poem:

> Functioning at the True Source of the Dharma
> Strengthening your roots
> The strong, saddled horse is already yours
> Be at peace on the journey of 10,000 miles

In 2009, Cuong left Plum Village and returned to lay life in the Netherlands, where in 2015 he received a master's degree in Buddhist Spiritual Care at Vrije ("Free") University in Amsterdam.

Cuong is the founder of Mind Only School, in Gouda, where he teaches Buddhist philosophy and psychology, specializing in Yogachara Buddhism combined with the Madhyamaka (Middle Way) School of Nagarjuna. Cuong leads retreats and gives Dharma talks in Europe, the US, and Asia, and offers presentations to large organizations. He is the author of four books in Vietnamese and one in Dutch. This is his first book in English.